The
AGONY
and the
ECSTASY

Designing Experiences For A Meaningful Life

Romasha Nath

Fern Express

Published by: Fern Express

ISBN: 979-8-9933305-1-8

Book Cover & Layout Design by: Abu Bakar Javed

Cover Image: African Southern Masked Weaver Bird, Adobe stock photo

To my virtuous and talented son,
Jeet Chakravarti

Contents

Acknowledgements

This book flowed from a wellspring of sixteen years spent in the trenches of entrepreneurship. The appliqué of prose and verse are tinged with flashbacks and memories. I have opened and shut two businesses in these years and survived the highs and lows, to share my experiences. This was possible because of the help, encouragement and guidance I have received from colleagues, clients, investors, advisors, educators and friends, Airbnb hosts who allowed me to stay when I found myself stranded in the aftermath of the pandemic, the list is long and loving. I hope someday to return the favor.

As the writer Don Roff likes to say, "writing means finishing. You can't improve, sell, captivate, or film what isn't done. So, finish the damn thing." I was able to complete *The Agony and the Ecstasy, Designing Experiences for a Meaningful Life*, thanks to my friend and colleague, Nancy Taylor and my advisor and client Ed Johnson, who kept my precious notes, books and personal effects secure in their homes through the long months of transition. A client who graciously included me in a workshop that brought me in touch with the finest leadership. Thank you, it was an honor—it meant I could reach the finish line. Thanks to my host Emmanuel Blackwood who allowed a long uninterrupted stay. Thanks to Oakland Coin & Jewelry Exchange for enabling me to create some immediate cash flow. I would like to thank my son Jeet, for being my best critic and cheerleader. Thanks to Abu Baker for his help with the formatting and design of the book. Finally, I would like to thank Oliver Arnoldi, an accomplished editor, writer and filmmaker. Oli has reviewed and guided this book—with every review he has made it a better book.

I owe more than I can say. Thank you everyone.

Introduction

My relationship with design began informally, often by hearsay. I drew from a deep well of imagination, to dismantle and examine stationary, common beliefs and reassemble them in ways that made sense to me. Creativity and design were interchangeable terms. I was guided by a sense perception, feeling my way and following interesting roads to arrive at a new destination of ideas, driven by a zest for life.

Midlife and many unanswered questions led me to return to school and study design through formal modes of inquiry. My thesis was framed as a contemporary design studio workshop, inspired by *disegno* of the Italian Renaissance, famous for thinking and making as an intellectual and sensualist pursuit. Although my inquiry did not lead me to a laconic definition of design, one that I found most appealing was Herbert Simon's oft-quoted declaration, "Everyone engaged in changing existing situations to preferred ones, is engaged in design." This view allows us to luxuriate and problem solve with the many possibilities for improvement, unlocked by design.

My progression as a *designisto* has me exploring design interventions to improve experiences in everyday life. An experience is an event or occurrence that is mainly felt and one that can leave an indelible mark on the outcome. Maya Angelou famously said, "I've learned that people will forget what you said, but they will never forget how you made them feel." In this book, I call attention to designing experiences that are intuitive and thoughtfully crafted.

This book is a medley of eleven essays—personal reflections informed by theory and practice. The insights dwell on some main events encountered by most people.

I worked through a wide-ranging portfolio to arrive at the eleven as my credo or philosophy of life. The book is not exhaustive yet distilled, it tells the truth without all the facts, provokes thought, and invites a conversation.

The essays have polythetic overlaps yet they are individually bound. Like songs on an album, tied by the common theme of love, they can be read in any order, creating a design consciousness for creating desirable experiences. The range covers the ephemeral and the enduring, the extraordinary and the banal, the agony and the ecstasy. Although the chapters are independent, you could say they flow to a poetic rhyme and meter, like the ebbs and flows of abab.

I share my learnings of over thirty years, enhanced by my study of design, in theory and practice. Experiences matter. Designing them with care helps us avoid pitfalls and creates room for quality. We dread experiences that are unsavory and avoid repeating them, even in memory. By calling attention to how we *experience the experience*, we improve the odds for a preferred outcome.

I share a few further readings, film snippets and podcasts towards the end to facilitate further reflection as we widen the circle for designing experiences.

ONE

Communication

"The single biggest problem in communication is the illusion that it has taken place." George Bernard Shaw was right. Designing the experience becomes supremely important for communication to be anything more than an illusion. The message, medium, context, space and, above all, listening for the heartbeat of the unsaid, where expression meets resonance, is how trust flourishes and negotiation stops. Few would dispute Aristotle's *Rhetoric* as an important guiding principle for communication. He defined rhetoric as "the art of observing in any given case the available means of persuasion." He espoused persuasion above manipulation as a basis for effective rhetoric. The persuasive powers of rhetoric cover a wider range than a dialectic, framed around a logical argument. Rhetoric is manifested by *ethos* (establishing credibility), *pathos* (appealing to the emotions of the audience) and *logos* (logic and reason that support the argument). These rubrics, conceived thousands of years ago by Aristotle, are rudimentary to a communication framework.

If we agree that persuasion is the most effective way to communicate, then feelings and what may be left unsaid, become more important than language or dialectics. Connecting with emotion, sometimes through nonverbal communication, can appeal to our senses in deeply persuasive ways. There is much written, purported and researched on this. Peter Drucker urges us to "hear what isn't said," and Maya Angelou's words have become idiomatic for our times: "People will forget what you said, people will forget what you did, but people will never forget how you made them feel." A short verse that appeals to me for its simple and poignant message reaffirms feelings more than words:

> When I speak
> Let not my words be all that is heard.
> Listen also to the feeling which borns them
> And allow that to correct any distortion
> Caused by the inaccuracy
> > Of my speech ~ Theta Burke

Jonathan Culler, the architect of the *Theory of Lyric* points out that we are predisposed to verse, particularly to making sense of nonsense. As children, we learn nursery rhymes before we learn to read, just as we learn to draw before we learn to write. Our emotions respond to such artforms and we learn to make sense of them, even believe in the nonsensical, before the rational. Why else would we still enjoy jingles like, "One for the money, two for the show, three to get ready, and four to go," with only a random link between the numbers and the accompanying words. We enjoy the jingle because it resonates with us at some intuitive level.

The way we communicate with animals is possibly the purest example of nonverbal communication that is reciprocal and well understood. In such communication, our tone, posture, energy and body language are more relevant than our library of words. Such a form of connection is known to foster human bonds as well. Of the many schools of thought in the humanities, poetry is one that appeals to our feelings the most. Poetry sits in the beautiful realm of literature with an arm's length from prose. It secures its spot as autonomous, without having to defend itself or offer facts in support of a claim. Facts become subordinate to feelings, yet because we experience poetry through our emotions it can be embedded in us for

5

its truth, devoid of the rational detail that can sometimes distance us from the essence of our humanity.

Poetry in the Public Realm

We experienced such a connection through the tragic lens of 9/11. A poem written by W. H. Auden, in a bar on 52nd Street in New York, titled "September 1, 1939", was what people turned to in the aftermath of 9/11. Auden composed this verse soon after Germany's invasion of Poland at the start of World War II:

> I sit in one of the dives
> On Fifty-Second Street
> Uncertain and afraid
> As the clever hopes expire
> Of a low dishonest decade:
> Waves of anger and fear
> Circulate over the bright
> And darkened lands of the earth,
> Obsessing our private lives;
> The unmentionable odour of death
> Offends the September night

Daniel Swift of *Times Literary Supplement* and *MSNBC* quoted liberally from this verse and said, "Auden's words are everywhere." People recited the verse in street corners and circulated it via email. Jonathan Culler, states that verse is unfettered by facts, we listen for why someone "speaks thus," or why someone "feels thus." Culler goes on to say that it would be unnatural for people to turn to a political or factual journal, the way they did to Auden's verse. It became cathartic and a source of comfort, to people across all callings in New York City and beyond. Poetry can operate beyond reason, free from the limits of the human mind. It allows us to "speak for the dumb," and "reach the deaf." Aside from the seduction of verse, Auden's poem served a public function after 9/11. As we delve deeper in the study of verse, Philip Sidney's reflection from *The Defence of Poesy*, "The poet, he nothing affirmeth, and therefore never lieth," can be interpreted as a verse being truthful without all the facts.

Of the many recitations of "September 1, 1939", one that appealed to me the most is by the actor, Michael Sheen. His style draws from emotion, as his tone, eyes and gestures articulate the words of this classic. The dramatic and sublime mode of delivery touches and persuades us. If feelings trump facts and the emotional supersedes the rational as a more effective form of communication, then designing the experience with care becomes a form for prepossessing outcomes.

Throughout my career I have found this to be a gap, whilst I've encountered the rational, I do feel we can be better at tuning into our poetic and intuitive side as we build logical arguments. Everyday life may not afford us a position to communicate in verse form, literally, yet we can figuratively embody our message such that it is felt and understood—why we "speak thus," or how we "feel thus."

Storytelling in Business

Verse, like melody, connects us to others at an emotional level. On a similar continuum, storytelling builds empathy when told with emotion. We put ourselves on the line when we share a personal story that could be moving. Storytelling in its oral tradition existed well before we learned to read and write. The visceral quality of a story has us engaged. Myth, skillfully fabricated and narrated, appeals to our senses. We follow the story arc if it strikes a resonance with us. Business stories can be dry and veer towards information and presentation. The essence of communication is creating human connection, information is secondary to forming a bond of trust. I sought to blur the lines between business narratives and storytellers from the social sciences. Buttressed by several years spent listening to personal stories of leaders and everyday professionals, I studied our native roots of storytelling through the lens of anthropology while at design school in New York. As part of an academic cohort, we created six prototypes. These prototypes were launched throughout the COVID 19 pandemic and found a resonance with the executive community, mainly unaware of such modes of storytelling. Given the popularity of this approach, I have since used these figures in my practice to stimulate narratives and build engagement—they continually add color to dry business presentations. After all, what good is a business story, if it cannot stir our primal, human interest and build motivation? I share the six archetypes from anthropology as references within the context of a business setting.

Shamanic Storytelling

Shamanic Storytellers are known for their healing powers. They balance vision with roots, light with shadow, through equanimity and playful wisdom. The connection between nature and the indigenous people, makes this form of storytelling therapeutic. It offers avenues to commune with the environment and life on the planet. Anthropologist Angeles Arrien, in her book, *The Four-Fold Way,* shares insights about healing in the Shamanic tradition. A Shamanic healer is primarily a storyteller and when treating an illness, pursues the following course of inquiry:

> When did you stop singing?
> When did you stop dancing?
> When did you stop being enchanted by story?

> When did you stop finding comfort in the sweet,
> territory of silence?

Such approaches could have special significance when building engagement or furthering wellness within a community. Story as a tool for healing has wide ranging application, particularly in personal development and turnaround situations that may be engulfed in a depressive, low morale.

Griot

The Griots of West Africa are storytellers who are historians, ambassadors, musicians, interpreters. A griot is assigned as the keeper of keys for rituals in the community. There is no one word that describes the full range of a Griot's function. Their storytelling is styled as praise singing rooted in historic accounts. Griot narratives involve memory and remembrance. The profession follows the legacy of father to son, with archives mainly passed down through verbal accounts; cheerleading leaders and chiefs who are part of the tribe in communal ceremonies are at the center of a Griot's storybook. Old tales are retold and new ones are added to the archives. I have found such a storytelling medium to be particularly relevant in environments where there is a need to revive tradition through pride and a sense of belonging.

Rakugo

The Japanese Rakugo storyteller is prominent for humor and entertainment. A Rakugo performance is styled as a parody, boisterous and theatrical. The orator can use a fan or kerchief and other props and ornament to exaggerate the message; douce something unsavory with humor, akin to a Shakespearean clown. The Rakugo breaks traditional lines of hierarchy to lighten an otherwise formal structure. Rakugo is particularly relevant in hierarchical situations where tensions and conflicts may be eased through a humorous enactment. Prickly issues can be raised in a light-hearted tone, difficult to broach or confront, otherwise. Rakugo could also serve as a precursor to a more formal conversation.

Pingtan

The Chinese tradition of Pingtan is eminent for its diplomacy and political stratagem. Pingtan storytelling continued in China despite communist victory in 1949, partly because some forms of culture were allowed to persist inspite of the cultural revolution. Besides, storytelling in its oral tradition was hard to rein in. Pingtan offers a framework to discuss traditional and contemporary issues. This form of storytelling can be effective in navigating political environments, passive aggressive cultures, a dialogue between business and bureaucracy, settings where confrontation could mitigate effectiveness. The cultural backdrop of Pingtan suggests manipulation through story to gain control. The form blends softness with authority, the yin and the yang.

Baul

The Baul is a form of troubadour from east Bengal, India. Traditionally a nomad, described as a wandering minstrel in folk culture. Their narratives cover folk tales often fabricated on the spot with compositions speaking of historic and contemporary social issues. The form can be exaggerated and profusely emotional with a high-pitched delivery style. An article in the Guardian by William Dalrymple titled, *The Song of the Holy Fools,* shares that Baul storytellers are non-conformist, social rebels, mystics who are believers of Sufi and Tantric traditions. The self-styled, inventive Baul invites debate by mocking the conventional. This style of storytelling is particularly relevant in unorthodox environments such as a high growth start-up that may be disrupting the status quo.

Seanchai

The quintessential Irish storyteller embodies myth and legend. The role was constructed to rely heavily on memory. The Seanchai was expected to memorize and recite stories, poems from history, in keeping with social rank, mainly for the praise and entertainment of the ruling class and nobility. The aristocratic patronage fell apart with the fall of the Gaelic order yet storytelling remained an enduring tradition. It lives on in a more informal sense through oral form, mainly for entertainment. Present-day storytelling in Ireland still draws from tradition but without the constraints of social reverence. The emphasis is on creativity and enchantment. Memory continues to play an important role in the narratives coupled with showmanship and folk style oratory. With its emphasis on entertainment and showmanship, such form of storytelling is relevant when shaping or spreading culture, sprucing a celebration, adding flair to the marketing campaign, among several other possibilities.

Stories viewed through a cultural lens offer a kaleidoscope of openings for expression, like Joseph's coat of many colors. When we style stories closer to our native roots, our primal instincts of sitting by a campfire or viewing a tale on a rustic stage are stimulated. It creates an interest beyond routine information that business leaders are accustomed to sharing in an already overcrowded world of information with fragmented attention spans. This approach brings a refreshing change. Designing a story experience for better communication can include a bouquet of options such as: anecdote, myth, fable, parable, folklore, satire, fiction, visioning, imaging, short stories, speech, jokes, acts, tales, scripts, farce, urban legend, oral recounts, and fireside stories or poems. Some common themes expressed through these storytelling modes are vindication, sacrifice, fear, fate, innovation, transformation, celebration, courage, justice, authority, tradition, remorse, friendship, respect, competition and rivalry. All of these can be adapted to create an outlet and reception for emotions.

A persuasive approach to communication, leading with feelings can be designed in harmony with the rational and the logical. A convergence can make the experience credible and build trusting bonds. The heart and mind, together, form a perfect balance.

Communication in the era of AI

Our lives have changed dramatically with AI. There could be clearer boundaries between the medium and the message, with the option to choose the medium most appropriate for our message. And yes, the choice of medium can overpower the message, thus Marshall McLuhan's sage call-out that the medium is the message. Without guardrails, AI can conceive, compose and convey the message without the human touch of feelings. Convenience can overtake care. Where would that leave our argument of leading our communication with the persuasive touch of poetry and story?

I am not a luddite yet I cannot help but reflect that these could easily become the worst of times for communication without the boundaries that preserve human connection. The emotional and rational can converge if we place our priorities in such a way that we lead with feelings and let rational and technological advancements facilitate the underlying belief that people only remember how we make them feel. Designing the experience for such an outcome matters more today than it ever did, we need to cut through the clutter to reach beyond the surface. Leading with emotions helps us connect to our common humanity and makes us more receptive to rational arguments:

> Once upon a time
> Thoughts and feelings
>> Lived in different rooms
> Not comfortable with each other
> You helped me learn
>> I could open the doors ~ Theta Burke

We are at a tipping point where our strides can be extended, where words can become vessels for the message set forth from the heart. Our transformative journey on the yellow brick road would be without a destination if we allow an artificial, passive flow of information—devoid of human connection—to cloud and distract us from true communication that can influence positive change.

A medium such as AI may have acquired power over the message, and consequently become the message. Does such passive acceptance of the medium perpetuate the medium's manipulative influence in our lives?

In our increasingly gender neutral world, effective communication takes a female form. Regardless of the medium, our sensitive human hand must hold the key to unlock the doors between the rational and the emotional if we aspire to be heard, to be influential and to be remembered. It is evident that our approach to communication with a verse and story mindset distinguishes the experience in our hypermediacy ridden present. Yuval Noah Harari, an acclaimed futurist, historian and technologist, warns of a dystopian future if we allow AI to march us into a totalitarian data-driven regime. We need to touch one another in special ways, through feelings. Auden's words continue to be everywhere:

> Of each woman and each man
> Craves what it cannot have,
> Not universal love
> But to be loved alone

This examination through the seams of verse and story offer influential paths for human connection. They help us move past the illusion that true communication has taken place. Designing the communication experience, with such a mindset, touches our feelings and gives us access to a deeper part of our common humanity. People always remember how we made them feel.

TWO

Goodbyes

Leave them laughing when you say goodbye—this popular refrain has echoed through time. Poets, songwriters, philosophers, littérateurs, civic and business leaders, jilted lovers, and disgruntled employees have all felt deeply about partings and the pain caused by goodbyes. Most of us would prefer to laugh than cry if a goodbye becomes inevitable. Yet few can say that they could laugh when disappointment bore them down. We are often at our best when we say hello and at our worst when we say goodbye.

A breakdown in a relationship that leads to a goodbye can sometimes give us a magnificent piece of literature such as Ernest Hemingway's *A Farewell to Arms,* widely known to have been inspired by his unrequited love for Agnes von Kurowsky. We can rise to the challenge of a goodbye and experience a Jerry Maguire moment, applauding the solidarity of the charming, sports agent's partner when she says, "You had me at hello," and cheer on his client, Rod Tidwell, who made possible the warm fuzzy, happy ending to Cameron Crowe's beloved 1996 film. These are just two examples where goodbyes contributed to grand accomplishments. Although Jerry Maguire is a fictitious character, his persona is inspired by Leigh Steinberg, a real life sports agent.

We are conditioned to celebrate the hero's journey triggered by a goodbye. Pain is seen by many as a way to grow and can sometimes lead us to our best work. The idea that great art comes from great pain is a widely debated subject, as is the concept of the tortured artist. There is a romance to painful partings and a longing for what could have been. Such sentiment can move us deeply and find a sublimated voice through expression, be it in the arts or in business. Although we do not speak of personal and business breakdowns in the same breath, particularly romantic breakdowns and professional farewells, I view them both through the lens of feelings. If we care deeply, we will hurt deeply in both instances. The heart does not distinguish between the various highways that lead us to pain. One of the most moving, and possibly the most romantic, goodbyes on celluloid is the farewell scene between Rick and Ilsa in the legendary film *Casablanca:*

Ilsa: And I said I would never leave you!
Rick: And you never will. But I've got a job to do too.
        Where I'm going you can't follow. What I've got
        to do you can't be any part of Ilsa. I'm no good at
        being noble, but it doesn't take much to see that the
        problems of three little people don't amount to a hill
        of beans in this crazy world.
        Someday you will understand that. Not now.
        Here's looking at you kid.

Channel this dialogue through the beautiful, teary-eyed Ingrid Bergman, and the dashing, tough yet kind Humphrey Bogart. Add the rain, and the circumstance of the course of true love being cruelly interrupted, and we have a masterpiece that never ceases to move us. What appeals to us in this drama is the emotional connection, the responsibility, and, above all, Rick's caring—he wishes to see Ilsa safe, and the oft-quoted line "Here's looking at you kid," is embalming. We feel cathartic, sad, and comforted. A painful parting can be etched in memory forever, the experience needs to be carefully folded and unfolded.

If we are fortunate, in our lifetime our hellos will outnumber our goodbyes, yet it would be inconceivable to think that we would be spared a few very painful partings that could be defining for us in their own unique way. "Happy families are all alike; every unhappy family is unhappy in its own way." I connect deeply with this opening line in Tolstoy's novel, *Anna Karenina*. I find this observation to hold true for most forms of unhappiness, events that cause us deep pain occupy a uniquely distinguished place in us, unlike say holidays that can all compile into a happy scrapbook of memories. Navigating such painful moments may call upon all the skills and resources we can muster. Until we can learn to translate the experience in some meaningful way, it can reside in us as an unwelcome roommate. The bigger question for those who initiate the goodbye is, "Why not leave them laughing when you go?"

That's No Way To Say Goodbye

There is an age-old notion that there is no nice way to communicate bad news. Being too smooth can be seen as slick and in some cultures this may be considered disingenuous. In a romantic alliance the partner who initiates the goodbye may take a particularly harsh stance despite being kind, because they are awkward and also because they may fear that being nice can send a misleading message of hope, when they actually want to leave the relationship. An old Diana Ross song shares such emotions well:

> There's no easy way to hear the words
> I'm sorry, I don't love you
> You tried to leave me once before
> But felt so bad you let me love you more
> And maybe there's no gentle way
> No tender sentimental way
> To leave me

Even when there may be a good reason for the breakup, if the other side does not wish to leave or may be unprepared for the departure, the responsibility to handle the exit thoughtfully may rest with the side initiating the move. It is a good position to take, respectful of what may have been a precious bond for a period of time. A simple, humorous take from Winnie-the-Pooh, a childhood favorite, says it well: "How lucky I am to have something that makes saying goodbye so hard?" If both sides take a view that they are fortunate that someone cares enough not to go and the one being left feels fortunate that they had something special they don't want to lose, then such a realization itself can be reassuring. Of course, this assumes that the parting is painful and that both sides are not pleased to leave. Indifference is seldom a foundation for a relationship. If there was a meaningful connection and one side initiates the goodbye, then the initiator holds most of the responsibility for a thoughtful transition.

The same argument can hold true for a business alliance that breaks down, regardless of contractual obligations. Ironically, some big companies accused of ruthless business practices are known to be quite good with overcompensating and leaving them laughing as they go. In the nineties, General Electric, Hewlett Packard, IBM, and several other Fortune 500 companies encouraged severances in times of plenty, to allow attractive exit packages. At senior levels, departures were sweetened and one could leave with a good handshake. The tradition of personalized communication, of well-designed hand-written messages, was an attempt to safeguard the reputation of both sides. The exits of our times have taken on a worrying impersonal trend. The severance does not amount to much and the message can come in the form of an impersonal email. The approach does not breed loyalty nor reputation. With the exception of businesses that are deep in the red or start-ups that may have folded, departures may need as much care as welcome packages. The obvious question becomes: does commitment, loyalty, and reputation matter for these companies? If there was a semblance of any relationship, then making exits as graceful as entries can only serve an organization well. It could be a predictable way within the company's grasp to earn a good reputation and become a preferred place to work.

Partnership breakdowns that lead to farewells in business can be equally painful and messy, often settled in court. The silver lining here is that everyone involved in a promising venture gets rewarded at some level. The McDonald brothers may not have enjoyed the same rewards as Ray Kroc yet they were bought out of the small business they ran and earned from the scaling by Kroc—less than they may have wanted but more than they would have earned without Kroc's intervention. Besides, their name became an American icon. A less famous example is Jimmy Choo, the shoemaker from Malaysia. Tamara Mellon scaled his small business, conflicts grew, and ultimately Jimmy Choo left to start his own venture, yet Tamara made him famous and he was financially rewarded. Jimmy Choo became a recognized global brand, a steep evolution after starting as a cobbler for the British aristocracy. The phenomenal success of Facebook caused friends who accused Zuckerberg of stealing their idea, to profit from what could have otherwise been a dorm room pipedream. Doers are usually rewarded in a business that does well and the winner ends up compensating the one they bid goodbye to, usually beyond what they were earning for an idea-waiting-to-happen or as an unknown entity with unassuming revenue.

Breaking Bad News

It was raining incessantly during Chinese New Year in Singapore. It was January of 2004 and I was taking a walk down Cornwall Gardens to do my usual weekly shopping in the Holland Village market. My cellphone rang. It was my mother, in a high-pitched tone, she said,

"Vick is no more."

Shocked, I said, "What?" She repeated the same message.

"He passed away at his family home last night from fever and pneumonia," and she hung up. Vick was my former husband and father of my son. Although we had parted ways some years ago, the news hit me like a blow. I remember crying all the way in the rain to Holland Village and finding a chair in a cafe to sit down and gain my composure. I was deeply pained. Our marriage was dysfunctional and had ended several years ago. Yet I felt deep remorse and guilt. I felt responsible, despite having done all I could to part responsibly. It took me a long time to understand that we have an obligation for our own well-being as adults, yet I continued to soul search if I could have done more, while preserving my own life and our son's future. I was haunted by the question, what more could we have done to save this, if anything? My otherwise caring mother, who was very upset by the news, assumed I was strong and hurled the message in two sentences with little regard for where I was at that time. It was the first time I had handled bad news of such magnitude alone. The rest of Chinese New Year and beyond lay heavy with mourning. I was fortunate to have the support of colleagues when the office reopened after the break. This may be an extreme example of receiving bad news, I share it because it is important to remember that we can sometimes underestimate the shock that people may experience when they receive adverse news.

Disengagement is a painstaking process in relation-ships that are more than superficial or transactional alliances. There is no such thing as too much care when it comes to a smooth separation. I would go so far as to say that engagement or the start of a relationship, where we are dealing with all positivity, the honeymoon phase, is already set for success, even with fractional effort on our part. Whereas disengagement is mainly set for failure by its very nature. Without thoughtful consideration of how, when, where and what we communicate, it could come back to haunt us in many different ways, not least due to our own enquiring conscience. The reward from careful unfolding of disengagement may begin with avoiding missed steps, with attentiveness to feelings and dispelling the distress that may follow from the bad news. We can aspire to turn disengagement into opportunity with high engagement and support. It is counterintuitive to do so and very few people do this. By going the extra mile, we create opportunity and strengthen our ties even as we say goodbye. Such an outlook may not always be applicable, yet worthy of exploration.

Most business exits done right may actually be welcomed by the one being asked to leave. They get some financial support and may be able to pursue paths that they would not have been able to take otherwise, like going back to school possibly, or paying off the mortgage on their home, or taking a gap year in Europe alongside so many other possibilities. In other situations, an ill-timed departure could be catastrophic. What can be helpful is open, thoughtful communication. Some may take a severance and leave, others may take healthcare and some support with accommodation. In other situations, it may not be out of turn to sponsor a small business or a nonprofit for someone seeking a career pivot, and in many cases it is common practice for former employees to transition into contractual roles, given their under-standing of the company. There are many ways in which a company can leave them laughing as they go, so to speak, by personalizing the disengagement with open, heartfelt communication.

Overcompensating in personal breakups when you are causing pain to someone who may have mattered, is an appropriate remedy. If you take something, give something—it is decent and makes the departure more agreeable. Wealthy partners are known to offer financial rewards akin to business exits, and there are ways that not so wealthy partners too can overcompensate—with time, errands, committed responsibilities, a lifelong friendship, and reframing the old relationship.

It is seldom only about money or other forms of compensation. Taking all factors into account serves as an assurance and a way forward. The old-fashioned belief that talented and capable individuals can find a way mainly holds, but factors outside one's control can play a role. Cultural realities of midlife, be it a personal challenge or a professional one, can become daunting even for those who may be capable. Overcompensating and being thoughtful with transitionary support in material ways is kind and appropriate. Generosity and thoughtfulness can never be bad investments in a breakup. It is the poverty of spirit and lack of thoughtfulness that can make a parting even more painful than it needs to be. Always have the patience to leave them laughing when you say goodbye. The original architect of the expression, George Cohan, offers some playful wisdom. I bid you to read it with the intention to lighten the heaviness of a departure. A joke may be untimely, but humor and friendship is always timely:

> Always leave them laughing when you say goodbye
> Never linger long about or else
> you'll wear your welcome out
> When you meet a fellow with a tear-dimmed eye
> You can leave him laughing if you try
> When he tells his troubles interrupt him with a joke

Tell him one he's never heard and
he'll declare that it's a bird
When he's giggling good you know
That's the time to turn and go
Always leave them laughing when you say goodbye

Designing the Departure

Before we rush to design an exit communication, it may help to revisit why the person was special to you, their virtues, and what led to the breakdown. Such a reflection will help tailor the exit equitably. It may also surface qualities you may not wish to lose in the whirlwind of immediate priorities. Seeds for the future can emerge. You may wish to retain their services in another form, or reframe the professional alliance into a new chapter. If this is a departure from a personal relationship, you may discover that you still continue to share a passion for the arts, sports or whatever drew you to one another beyond pure romance. If indeed, it was romance only, then perhaps you now have an added seat at some annual dinner parties, possible fundraisers, and charities. Investments in relationships are important and unless it is an outright case of treason or corruption, they may be worthy of re-evaluation and reframing.

The space where you break the news is important. People remember such defining moments. Pick a place that is calm, tasteful, and in keeping with the context. Keep it simple yet elegant. You do not want to break such news in a busy cafe or the office, and a fancy lunch may be too much. A private, neutral setting where both sides are on equal footing, can create a better opening and exchange. Booking a private room at a business center or club could offer privacy and neutrality. Share events that led to the decision and macro-drivers. Listen to responses with care. If it is *fait accompli*, be clear right away so the conversation can move to the future. It may help not to turn this into a performance review if the intention is to move on— this holds true of both personal and professional conversations. A review is best if the desire is to fix problems and stay. Otherwise, positivity and wishes for a good future are a better approach. Explain what you can offer and how you arrived at it. Be nice but this is not the time to negotiate. Steer the conversation towards a thoughtfully designed closure that compensates for the parting and is protective of the individual's future. The more care and empathy there is, the better the chances of a smooth departure. Share personal examples. Have a couple of choices—financial, in kind, and any other form of asset. Offer a series of openings over a week or ten days to enable clarifications and understanding. In the case of personal breakups, it could take a month or two, or more, to adjust emotions.

Most people come under a cloud and see doom and gloom when bad news is communicated but if they see a bright future then not only does the hurt settle, they may actually start to enjoy conversations about the next chapter. Imagine telling your partner that you will sponsor them for that special course or business, or if money is not an issue, buy them a small apartment in their favorite city, or a holiday—something that makes them happy at whatever level of expense you can afford. It is a better way than a blunt, "I'm in love with someone else," or "we're hiring someone who meets our needs." Be sensitive. The more preparation, homework, and care you can take, the more likely a preferable closure and the possibility of a friend for life. Charisma, honesty, future-facing humanness, improves the odds for someone signing on the dotted line.

Where there is en masse exit, there may be less at stake, yet keeping it framed as a personal meeting allows for pleasantries and a handshake, impossible to accomplish on a Dear All email. Exit roads can be thorny, despite our best efforts. If the bar is set for a relationship that has a future, at least at some human level, then there can be light despite what may appear to be anguish in the present moment. A well-designed experience could lead to everyone welcoming the change.

I came upon this nice note that takes the sting away from communicating disappointing news. Although not a direct fit to a departure communique, the personalized touch and focus on gains, rather than losses, creates a positive message. A similar tone, designed to the context of a departure, delivered personally, can allow the recipient grace and something to share with their family. It is important to remember that families are always impacted by such developments. In the case of a departure from a personal relationship, the message could be a well composed, loving letter.

To: George Neruda
From: Alex Tran

George, you may have heard rumors, but I want to personally tell you that Greta Gables is being promoted to SVP finance, starting November 19.

I also want to take the opportunity to tell you how much we appreciate the extraordinary way you do your job, it hasn't gone unnoticed. Your marvelous tutelage of Greta, bringing her along to more and more responsibilities made it possible for her to be selected for this spot. You will have a good friend in her.

You are probably wondering why you didn't get the position.

George, you have spent so many years in finance that moving a notch higher would mean no new challenge for you. You would be doing the same thing, only under more pressure. There is little difference in pay. We have you in mind for other important assignments both within and outside the finance function.

Financially, you will be doing well, too. You've been here a long time and have accumulated a nice nest egg. And you can expect a 10 percent raise in your next paycheck as an expression of our appreciation of your work.

I know you will cooperate with Greta all the way in this transition. Please give my best wishes to Emma and your children Peter and May.

> With best wishes,
> *Alex Tran*

At various times in our lives, we will have to say goodbye, and may find ourselves as bearers of bad news. It is in these moments that we can truly shine if we put ourselves in the shoes of the receiver and design a farewell attuned to how they may like to receive such news. Leaving them laughing can be the best, most compassionate policy.

THREE

Kintsugi

I walked through Central Park. It was early autumn in New York and the air was crisp, with the leaves starting to turn yellow and amber—a harbinger of change. I preferred to walk through the park instead of walking on Columbus Avenue, reengaging my senses, through central park, away from the library and desk. The earthy, slightly musty smell from leaves mingled with the nutty, roasted coffee notes from my to-go cup. Scent memory never leaves me, it never fails to bring a rush of expectancy, particularly with changing seasons. I agree with Kipling that smells can "make your heart-strings crack." I had reached the edge of the Upper West Side, and walked onto Amsterdam Avenue. I was visiting Dori-san at his studio, which was also his home. He had agreed to let me watch him repair a bowl as he explained the artform of Kintsugi.

The old brownstone was charming, still fitted with a patina from the Gilded Age. Brass tones against wood and glass led me up the stairs to the fifth floor. Dori-san, a frail, weathered man, greeted me at the door. A Japanophile, he had left his career in graphic design to devote himself to Kintsugi. A large drafting table with various pottery on one side was divided by a workstation on the other side, towards the window. His cat, a beautiful smokey grey Persian called Sir Toby, sat on the coach, greeting me with no more than a wink. I asked Dori-san why he chose a name from *Twelfth Night* for his cat—he explained that his ex-wife was an actress on Broadway. We sat by the workstation, with the melancholy notes of Eric Satie's "Gymnopédie No.1" in the background.

"*Kin* means gold in Japanese and tsugi means joining," he said softly. I sat down to an experience that became a learning for life. Dori-San went on to explain that lacquer is used to fill gaps after joining the broken pieces of pottery with adhesive, a coating of lacquer creates a glossy shine. The restoration highlights brokenness and blemishes, "We celebrate imperfections, it is about Wabi Sabi," he said sagely. Wabi Sabi, the philosophy behind celebrating imperfection, finds a perfect meeting in a Kintsugi-restored object. "This is an Oido, a tea bowl," Dori-san explained, it took about six months to restore, the bowl you just saw will dry for several days and will be burnished with lacquer many times so that it blends smoothly. As a final step, it will be dusted and polished with gold and silver, the gold and silver stick to the cracks, bringing life to the broken pieces." My gaze shifted from the work in progress to the restored Oido, in all its glory, the fractured parts stood out like golden branches of a tree on glaze. A medley of images, colliding with verse and thoughts contrasting eastern and western concepts, gushed through my mind. Like a rainbow of colors that fall on a wall when a ray of light passes through a prism. I was reminded of Keats' *Grecian Urn:*

> O Attic shape! Fair attitude! with brede
> Of marble men and maidens overwrought,
> With forest branches and the trodden weed;
> Thou, silent form, dost tease us out of thought
> As doth eternity: Cold Pastoral!
> When old age shall this generation waste,
> Thou shalt remain, in midst of other woe
> Than ours, a friend to man, to whom thou say'st,
> Beauty is truth, truth beauty,—that is all
> Ye know on earth, and all ye need to know

John Keats was moved by the beauty and timelessness of a classical Grecian Urn. He was set free to explore poetic fields of glory, uplifted by the craftsmanship of the urn despite the personal turmoil in his life. Keats could trust such beauty to be ever present, timeless and true.

The Grecian Urn and the repaired Oido are both an ode to beauty, the truth is where they differ. The Grecian Urn is about perfection and the Oido reflects beauty through imperfection. Kintsugi reveals and celebrates flaws, the object becomes more beautiful by highlighting and restoring flaws. Legend has it that Kintsugi has its roots in 15th century Japan, in the muromachi period. The shogun Ashikaga Yoshimasa was unimpressed by the repairs on a tea bowl while preparing for a tea ceremony and ordered a new, more aesthetic form of restoration, which led to the birth of Kintsugi. Dori-san explained the Japanese idiom *mononoaware,* literally translated as the pathos of things, the transience or a bittersweet passing and the ephemeral. By restoring the broken there comes a permanence and an acceptance of the transience. Dori-san shared that in restoring broken pottery, he restored himself and found beauty and acceptance through beautifying imperfection. The flaws in his relationships became endearing and forgivable in the unfinished pursuit of life. Beauty can be a progression, made beautiful with artistry and technique. A main learning from the studio was the technique of Kintsugi. It was applied perfectly, with precision, for the transformation of the broken and imperfect artifact. A perfect technique made the celebration of imperfection possible.

I was attracted by the form of Kintsugi, beyond its application to objects. I realized that Kintsugi could be a metaphor for relationships. What if we could celebrate the flaws of our friends and family, and restore relationships to become more beautiful like the Oido? What technique could we apply to restore the flawless beauty of our flawed relationships?

Breakdowns are inevitable. A quick read of countries, businesses and partnerships, suggests that conflicts and breakdowns are a part of our DNA. There is no chapter in history when we have been spared of this strife.

According to the U.S. Chamber's Institute for Legal Reform (ILR), costs and compensation in the U.S. tort system amounted to $529 billion in 2022. Approximately $16.5 billion is spent on divorce litigation each year in the US. These are mere statistics. When we add the cost of time, suffering, other invisible and opportunity costs, the figure becomes unquantifiable. Let us take the examination to mega grounds, what is the cost of war? It becomes unquantifiable. Measurements have their limitations, what we do carry with us is memory, feelings and experiences. These experiences are passed on by us as folklore.

If conflicts are inevitable should it lead us to a place of resignation? Why worry about something that is inevitable, accept *perimus,* we all perish? At every turning point we find inspiration from turnarounds, reconciliations, stories that gladden our hearts, we find a reversal, *gaudium vitae,* joy of life. Such joy always centers around relationships, repairs and newfound beauty. We cannot bypass breakdowns nor wish them away yet we can revel in the beauty of something more powerful, the transformation that comes from reconstruction and repairs. The influence of kintsugi as a guiding principle for relationships can be monumental.

My accidental realization of kintsugi in a broader sense dawned like a gestalt experience. I decided to investigate a few disparate situations that were imperfect, broken, sometimes unconventional, yet beautiful and enduring, when repaired, reframed and better realized. Below, I share some examples from entertainment, business, geopolitics and more intimate relationships. What I hope for you to see is that the concept of kintsugi can intervene almost anywhere as a benevolent spirit of restoration.

Banded by Harmony and Discord

Doheny Drive runs between Beverly Hills and West Hollywood. Driving down Doheny towards Santa Monica,
offers some iconic Los Angeles sights of streets lined with
palm trees and buildings in the Spanish Colonial Revival
style, further down on Santa Monica Boulevard stands
an unassuming two storied, grey building with a sign that
says Doug Weston's Troubador. This Nightclub is where
Glenn Frey, Don Henley, Bernie Leadon and Randy
Meisner, the founding members of the Eagles, played
frequently. The Eagles were formed in 1972 and rose to
fame for their harmonious, folk and soft rock songs like
Peaceful Easy Feeling:

> I like the way your sparkling earrings lay,
> Against your skin, it's so brown
> And I wanna sleep with you in the desert tonight
> With a billion stars all around
> 'Cause I gotta peaceful easy feeling
> And I know you won't let me down
> 'Cause I'm already standing
> On the ground

The Eagles are a masterclass for the Kintsugi-principle.
They embody all the traits that make breakdowns and repairs
beautiful with their inherent flaws and imperfections. The
band had a meteoric rise in the mid 70s, with tracks like
Hotel California, their *Greatest Hits* became the best selling
album of the 20th century. The band won five number-
one singles and six number-one albums in the US. They
also received six Grammy Awards. Yet under all the fame
and success there were ongoing conflicts. Glenn Frey
and Don Henley, the alpha males, assumed leadership for
the band, remarkably different in their approach. Frey,
ambitious and a proponent of rock, Henley a perfectionist
leaning on folk, they had creative differences, their egos

grew with the band's success, Bernie Leadon and Randy Meisner were often pushed over. Bernie Leadon, a country artist, was ousted from the band when he famously poured a beer over Glenn Frey's head, asking him to take it easy. The straw that broke the back was a performance in 1980 which triggered a fight backstage between Glenn Frey and Don Felder, who had joined the band in the mid 70s, the fight ended with Don Felder smashing his guitar against a concrete pillar offstage at the close of the show. Don Henley made the famous remark that the band would only ever reunite if Hell Freezes Over. Hell did freeze over, the Eagles reunited in 1994 with their best tour yet, *Hell Freezes Over*.

The Eagles story is bundled with contradictions. They are flawless on stage and combustible off stage. Their second act eclipses the first, they have been around for 30 years since hell froze over. Despite fights, departures, lawsuits and passings, they live on with new members, true to their composition. Deacon Frey has succeeded his father Glenn, a rare form of succession for a band. Irving Azoff has been their manager since the 70s. Their fans love them. They soldier on, perfectly imperfect and in sync.

A Fashion House Saga

"During the whole of a dull, dark, and soundless day in the autumn of the year, when the clouds hung oppressively low in the heavens, I had been passing alone, on horseback, through a singularly dreary tract of country; and at length found myself, as the shades of the evening drew on, within view of the melancholy House of Usher. I know not how it was--but, with the first glimpse of the building, a sense of insufferable gloom pervaded my spirit." Poe wrote about this over a hundred years ago, and may have said so again, this time for the Fall of the House of Gucci and the murder of Maurizio Gucci.

Lady Gaga's star performance in the film *House of Gucci* brought the Gucci story and luxury brand within the homes of everyday people. We could laugh, cry, experience melodrama and the comfort of our darling brand's resurrection. The intervention of cinema or the arts played an important role in engagement and inclusivity. Royalty like the Gucci family could be flawed. The gossamer and veneer was torn and tarnished from within. While some things can never be reversed, you cannot bring back Maurizio from the dead or it is unlikely that the daughters Allegra and Alessandra Gucci or Patrizia herself for that matter, would ever forgive Patrizia Reggiani for the murder of Maurizio Gucci. Yet despite the doom and gloom we can celebrate the piecing together and reconstruction of the legendary House of Gucci, formed in 1921 by Guccio Gucci.

Many hands played a role in the turnaround, Tom Ford, the creative director for ten years, was instrumental in lifting the brand from insolvency. Domenico De Sole who became CEO, steered the fashion house to a public offering in the mid 1990s, financial stability is the lifeblood in a turnaround, Investcorp, an investment firm stabilized Gucci by acquiring a large stake at the peak of the family's feuds. PPR, a French luxury conglomerate led by François Pinault, acquired a controlling interest and rescued Gucci from a possible hostile takeover by LVMH. Gucci continues to encounter ebbs and flows, yet the dark clouds could be weathered by capable, outsider intervention.

Much has been said about the dispassionate character of business. It is easier to merge, break up and come back together if it makes financial sense, devoid of feelings. In a recent conversation on Bloomberg Television, titled *Mergers, Breakups* and the *Battle for Content*, July 2025, the debate moved to content and talent. The spotlight shifted to those who make the magic and their contribution to business success. By giving agency to the performers who create the experience, a hypergolic effect can move the dialectic from commerce to include content, craft and connection, the propulsion creates enduring business value by pairing the rational with the emotional.

Geopolitics—Four Perspectives

Bloodshed and destruction from war leaves the deepest of scars. Mending the broken after a war and reestablishing trust and friendship is possibly the most challenging of all. Who could imagine that Israel and Germany could be friends, or that apartheid in South Africa would end, or that a reversal of power would make India the second biggest investor in Great Britain or that the IRA would lay down their arms. Yet these miracles have happened, *gaudium vitae* has an advantage over *perimus*. These are but a few examples from a grand ballroom of inspiration. The Kintsugi-effect brings artistic intervention to healing and restoration. The victor and the vanquished find outlets that sublimate pain towards poetry.

It took many relentless efforts by the Germans to win trust with the Jews after the end of WWII. A visceral act can move where words cannot travel. On Dec 7, 1970, twenty-five years after the end of WWII, German Chancellor Willy Brandt knelt before the memorial to the victims of the 1943 uprising of Jews imprisoned in the Warsaw Ghetto. The image became a symbol of peace and unity. An extract of Willy Brandt's genuflection and his words:

> I knelt in front of the monument to those who died
> in the Warsaw Ghetto, despite derisive comments in
> the Federal Republic, I am not ashamed of this act.
> I did what people do when words fail. In this way I paid
> tribute to the millions murdered.

Brandt was instrumental in the collapse of the Berlin Wall, he won the Nobel Peace Prize in 1971 and could see his vision for a unified Germany come to life before his death in 1992. Some of the praise bestowed on Brandt states that he reconciled Germans with themselves, he changed the relationship of Germans with the world. In this spontaneous act of genuflection, Brandt asked for forgiveness on behalf of the Germans for the crimes of the Nazi regime. This unexpected gesture gained him respect and could move people beyond words. The black and white photograph of Brandt kneeling down draws upon our emotions for its aesthetics, vulnerability and authenticity.

There are few experiences as visceral as sports in forging team spirit. Nelson Mendela was released from prison after twenty-seven years and took up office as the President of post apartheid South Africa in 1994. The 1995 Rugby World Cup was an opportunity to promote reconciliation after decades of racial divide between the black majority and white minority. Rugby was viewed as a white Afrikaners sport. Nelson Mandela saw the Rugby World Cup hosted by South Africa, as an opportunity to bring the country together and bridge the divide. Mandela embraced the Springbok symbol associated with the white minority. He met with the captain François Pienaar and shared his vision of unification. South Africa defeated New Zealand at the iconic match. Mandela presented the Webb Ellis Cup wearing a Springbok jersey with Pienaar's number 6 on it. The predominantly white crowd at the stadium erupted in cheers. It was a symbolic moment of unity for South Africa and a step towards national pride. The match inspired the Clint Eastwood film *Invictus*. Poetry and sport came together with the famous lines from the poem that have become synonymous with Nelson Mandela's persona. "I am the master of my fate, I am the captain of my soul."

It took Gandhi thirty-two years of struggle, along with other freedom fighters, to lead India to her independence in 1947. One of the best portrayals of this chapter of history is Richard Attenborough's 1980 film, *Gandhi*. The screenwriter John Briley and Attenborough could popularize the inspiring struggle through a moving biographical film that created awareness for India and captured the imagination of global audiences. Yet again, the authentic and artistic form moves us at a visceral level, particularly when Gandhi's resounding welcome in 1931 London, from Kingsley Hall, declaring, "Gandhi is here. The Indian Nationalist leader, whose personality is intriguing the whole world," is contrasted by Churchill's comment of Gandhi as a "half naked fakir." The turnaround relationship between India and Great Britain is perhaps the most inspiring. Not only are the wounds healed, there is active involvement of Indians in British politics and industry, with India as the second largest investor in Britain. The underpinnings of culture, history and the arts have blossomed into an enduring friendship, where historical breakdowns have become a source of jest and creative expression, as in the film, *Bend It Like Beckam* and either side's preoccupation with curry and cricket.

These examples are a leap to the past, what philosopher Walter Benjamin liked to call, *Tigersprung*, The Northern Ireland cultural bridge continues to be on a precipice. It presents an important lens for present day conflicts and the possible role of cultural and artistic interventions to speed up the road to friendship. The IRA formally ended its armed struggle by decommissioning its weapons in 2005. A win for diplomacy as it presents an example of peaceful coexistence within disagreements. The Sinn Féin and the British monarchy are as far as it can get in political ideology, yet recent gestures by Sinn Féin at the passing of Queen Elizabeth II and attendance at King Charles III's coronation are remarkable strides towards friendship. The charismatic Gerry Adams of Sinn Féin said it well when he acknowledged to King Charles III on his visit to Ireland, thirty years after the end of *Troubles* that "We don't have a huge amount in common with the British Royalty but at a human level and personal level both sides have suffered," it was time to end the conflict.

Mending the broken through experiences in the arts and sports leave an indelible mark, the inevitable Serengeti of emotions find a place of peace through the poetry of life.

Relationships that Endure

Study after study points to the importance of relationships as a driving force in our well being. A long running study by Harvard University found that the quality of our relationships has a powerful influence on our happiness. The study was conducted over 85 years and followed 724 men from adolescence to old age. The research revealed that people with strong, supportive relationships were happier, healthier, and lived longer than those with fragile or volatile relationships. It is evident that we can foster only a few trusting relationships or deep friendships in a lifetime, no more than four or five that endure extended periods of time.

Anthropologist Rubin Danbar suggests that we can maintain a circle of family and friends with as many as 120 - 150 people, this can form our village. Although having a big circle may offer us social anchors, we form intimate, trusting relationships with very few. A study by the Pew Research Center shares that a majority of US adults, up to 53%, have between one to four close friendships. Breakdowns of intimate, trusting relationships can be unquantifiable, too often, a breakdown results in a shut down, the baby goes with the bathwater.

The folklore of *Lancelot and Guinevere* from the legend of *King Arthur and the Knights of the Round Table* is an allegory for our times. The medieval romantic drama is enacted regularly in our relationships. The eternal triangle of affections, powerplay, the roundtable or command central, betrayal, rivalry and the quest for love. Navigating the gauntlet in the battlefield of hearts is a human preoccupation. We love and we often have to leave. We lose more than our hearts when a deeply meaningful relationship is severed. Lovers may start as friends but seldom do lovers become friends:

> I followed on foot, but my armour was so heavy that
> I made little progress, and I would have gladly torn off
> my helmet and plates, and thrown my shield away, except
> that a man cannot even unbuckle his armour by himself.
> Exhausted and weary, a man in iron clothes,
> I came at last to where you were, and killed your captors
> and set you free.
>
> Then I stretched out my arms like a little child and
> begged you to uncouple my harness and unlace
> my metal gloves.
> I knelt down and you lifted up my visor and kissed me.
>
> My armour off, it lay like an effigy of myself on the floor.
> I was naked with you, carapace of hero put aside,
> I was not Lancelot, I was your lover ~ Jeanette Winterson

Closer to our times, we know that Elizabeth Taylor may have married eight times with unattainable fulfillment, yet her alliance with Richard Burton was enduring despite upheavals, it evolved through a lifetime. Ironic as it may seem, few can lay claim to such continuity amid brokenness.

Fast forward to our times, Bill and Melinda Gates announced their divorce in 2021 and continued to co-chair the Bill and Melinda Gates Foundation until 2024. Bill Gates has announced that the Gates Foundation will close by 2045 after an accelerated pace of giving away approximately $200 billion. Although Malinda Gates has since resigned as co-chair, to pursue her own growth and philanthropic interests, the professional transition stands out as a rare example despite personal breakdowns. An ideal beyond their personal desires endured their amicable transition. To leave and stay in a meaningful way is a feat few have accomplished. The French term *savoir faire* does not have a nuanced English translation, other than the literal one, *knowing how to do*. The term may best characterize their position, compared to several other prominent breakdowns.

Simone de Beauvoir and Jean-Paul Sartre met as students in 1929. They shared an enduring partnership that lasted 50 years ending only with Sartre's death in 1980. They never married but stayed committed by choice, they shared a passion for philosophy, literature, and intellectual curiosity, they promoted each other's work, without rivalry or powerplay, the foundation of the relationship was respectful, honest and enduring.

Letters to Sartre has a troveful of letters that touch the pulse of their enduring bond. This note, a light everyday account says it all, at heart, they were good friends.

> I visited Vals, which is quite pleasant as spas go -
> perhaps partly due to the fact that it was only eight in
> the morning and the streets were empty.
> I swill lemonade
> which is exquisite in these parts, being made
> precisely from Vals water. I eat one enormous meal
> daily, which is sometimes very good but always
> accompanied by dreadful wine, and one
> small cold meal. I have plenty of money and
> live very well.
> Do you know the story of Ortega and the bull? Or
> the one about a strangely invigorating hair dye?
> Remind me to tell you them,
> And also to tell you about a certain boy scout.

There are pinball machines everywhere I go, and
once or twice I've almost been tempted
to play. ~ S. de Beauvoir

Relationships is a sloppy word, it can mean everything or nothing. Friendship is the most noble and enduring of alliances. Friendships can exist in business, among nations, in a family and with anyone who befits such a space. Friedrich Nietzsche's *aphorisms on love and hate* state that the foundation of a successful marriage is the ability to be good friends. A lack of friendship, rather than a lack of love, is often what leads to unhappy marriages. This view may hold true beyond marriage. We may be quick to judge those who view relationships as friendships to be unconventional, when in fact such a road may be the most enduring and withstand the changing fortunes of time.

Mending relationships or transitioning them to a place of friendship can be possible when we draw inspiration from the Kintsugi-principle. My use of this term is metaphorical, similar to other theories such as the Goldilocks-principle. Through its use, I endeavor to open vistas of beautiful possibilities of mending the old or broken, in perfectly new ways. The technique we apply, allows us to celebrate imperfections, allowing comfort of the old with excitement of discovery. Dori-san enjoyed mending the bowl, for in doing so, he mended himself. As we think of our best friendships we will find we enjoyed something in our experience with them. It could be a shared interest or purpose, an activity we enjoyed together or their company may have attracted us. These experiences are mainly asexual and could form the reason to reposition the relationship within the space that brought us some form of pleasure. If the relationship was one of colleagues, there could be even more areas of connection to revisit. Time can be our most precious commodity, and a redesign of banked, predictable, shared experiences can offer a springboard for new beginnings.

FOUR

Style

The response to a quick internet search when you type "stylish" leads us to fashion, and a search for the term "style" offers an explanation that speaks of "a manner in which something is expressed or performed." Fashion stands for a popular trend. Someone who follows fashion may not have style and someone who is stylish may not be fashionable.

Three well-known personalities drive this point home: Pablo Picasso is known for his legendary artistry and style yet he mainly wore his signature blue-and-white-striped marinière, the remarkably gentle style of Mother Theresa is marked by the blue stripes on a voile sari with which she covered her head. Likewise, Gandhi's trademark saddle bridge eyeglasses and lucid oratory were relatable to the common man. All three did not follow fashion but had a distinct style. There is a clear distinction between style and fashion, even though we often use the terms interchangeably.

Style covers almost everything we do or say, and a conscious style is bred from self-awareness. The most stylish individuals reflect authentic characteristics of their personality and beliefs through their style palette. The outward manifestation of style could be apparel but we soon realize that communication, philosophy, likes, dislikes, lifestyle, personal attitudes and so much more encompasses style. *Le style c'est l'homme meme* ("the style is the man himself"), an important insight by the 18th century natural scientist George Louis, Comte de Buffon lends clarity to the overarching relevance between style and how we engage with the world. We can develop an unconscious style like an unkempt garden but a conscious, authentic style is one we cultivate from the depths of self-awareness.

A signature style at a cosmetic level, mimics personal taste and demeanor. Anne Slater, a New York socialite, would wear blue cobalt-tinted sunglasses all the time, indoors or outdoors, day or night, at a casual event or a black tie gala. Known for her refined taste, she exuded Old World glamour and wit. She is known to have quipped, "A woman needs four animals in her life: a mink in the closet, a Jaguar in the garage, a tiger in bed and an ass to pay for it all." Slater resides amongst the best dressed in *Vanity Fair's* Hall of Fame.

The musician Dizzy Gillespie's style spoke of rebellious bebop era entertainment. His trumpeting trademarks were his puffy cheeks, horn-rimmed glasses, beret, and improvisation. He is known to have played with a bent trumpet because he discovered a broken sound quality from it that was better than the sound from a perfect trumpet. Dizzy's style can be described as more storied than cosmetic because he embodied his craft in it.

Style in the Public Realm

The style of public figures resonate a keen sense of cultivated authenticity. They evolve from where they come from to build bridges towards where they want to go and who they serve. They open conversations with various constituents or stakeholders with their style. John F. Kennedy's style conveyed a youthful and relaxed sophistication. His slim-fitting tailored suits and relaxed casualwear, rolled-up sleeves, and untucked shirts gave him an approachable charismatic air. He is known to have relaxed the design of the Oval Office, he championed the astronauts, and embraced the media and pop culture. He became a style icon with American families, creating a charming style with an air of "effortless cool."

The more conservative Margaret Thatcher was known for her signature power dressing in the 80s. She was not a trendsetter and worked hard to build political and cultural boundaries with her style. She has famously said, "Who do I dress for?" Daniel Conway of the University of Westminster shares that Thatcher's conscious attention to clothes mirror both constraints and agency of "actors in the public realm." With no precedence of female leadership to refer to, Thatcher's position was considered transgressive, she performed her gender with ambivalence and assertion, colored by her political persona and dramatized by her image as the "Iron Lady." Thatcher could wear many masks to parlay her position—this included a choice of colors such as "Washington Pink," "Peking Black," or "Kremlin Silver." Thatcher's style evolved from a provincial upbringing to political fame via Oxford. To connect with her conservative constituents, she softened her look with pussy bow blouses even when they clashed with her assertive power suits. She could relate with men and women, keeping to a style of an iron hand in a velvet glove.

Style in Business

Unlike socialites, entertainers, or political personas, business leaders have the challenge of working within the boundaries of their corporate culture and title, even as they may need to send an individually crafted message of confidence and credibility through their style.

Christine Lagarde, President of the European Central Bank, represents solid French bourgeoisie, raised in a devout Roman Catholic family in Normandy. Despite what may appear to be a privileged upbringing, her success has been attributed to hard work, competence, and an individual streak. Lagarde has broken the glass ceiling more than once in her career. Diane Johnson of *Vogue* shares that her style reflects an "outsider's credibility" in a world of men. Johnson adds that the French political elite labeled her "too elegant"—despite the odds, she became successful. Her style is elegant and assertive, she kept the title of Chairman while at the law firm Baker McKenzie with the formal salutation of Madam Chairman, instead of changing it to Chairwoman. Her suits are Chanel and lesser known brands like French, Ventilo, and the British Austin Reed, the latter known to be travel-proof attire as it does not crease easily. Her effective use of scarves tell a story that can be interpreted as bourgeois and bohemian. Robb Young of the BBC has commented that Lagarde fine-tunes her suits by wearing her scarves in many different ways— twisted, folded, wrapped, looped, double-knotted, or even intertwined with a string of pearls. Lagarde conveys a non-conformist streak through a seemingly inconsequential silk scarf. An asymmetrical knot is seldom part of a conventional style template.

Jamie Dimon, Chairman and CEO for JP Morgan Chase, has been cited as a best-dressed CEO. His suits are classic, tailored, and understated. He has confessed to wearing Ermenegildo Zegna suits for over thirty years. Dimon combines his suits with colorful silk ties and bold cufflinks—the only place in his attire for creative expression is the bold architecture of his cufflinks. His style is shaped by the rules of a senior executive who holds the interest of various stakeholders. There is a calm refinement to his demeanor, his leadership style is acknowledged for being intuitive and competent. He has worked through a complex maze of approaches to secure the bank through tumultuous times. He has been likened to Wellington at Waterloo for his strategic vision and operational excellence. Dimon's style has been studied, sliced and diced by scholars, likening his mindset to a "wartime CEO." Dimon's style comes together as classic, cool and collected.

Is There Power in the Suit?

The timeless film *The Godfather* provides a rich tapestry for the enactment of style. The power suit in the film is symbolic of intimidation, manipulation and seduction. The film draws from the Sicilian Mafia of New York City during the Great Depression of the 1930s. The times called for skills that could navigate survival and scarcity with cunning. Those who did not join a gang or operate as Mafia were excluded, left to suffocate and die. The outer manifestation of style in the dapper suits worn by Marlon Brando and Al Pacino are combined with refined and intimidating language. The film is peppered with statements that are oft-quoted to this day, in situations that demand powerplay, like "I made him an offer he could not refuse." This line effectively implies a gun held to the head, where saying "no" meant death. The dichotomy between lawmaker and outlaw is a running theme in the film, the killing becomes virtuous in the name of territory and as self-defense for family and business interests. The violence is never eccentric or whimsical. There is a stylistic tension that runs throughout the film, a code, be it in attire or manner. The film has served as a metaphor for control in business, with the violence sublimated as competition. Style characteristics similar to *The Godfather* are enacted everyday, metaphorically in business through hostile takeovers and negotiations that lead to mergers and acquisitions, where saying no may not be an option. *The Godfather* serves as an example of how a well-defined style can become a means for survival through control, power, and manipulation.

Anne Hollander, historian and author of *Sex and Suits,* offers remarkable insights on the suit as it intersects with everyday style. She distinguishes between sexuality and seductiveness. Sexuality marks the foundation for form, says Hollander's. The basic sexuality of the suit cannot be dismissed, even as it disengages from seductiveness. She draws a parallel between the suit and nature. "Panthers and gazelles" wear easy-fitting suits with natural grace and all shapes and sizes fit well in nature. The suit provides our body with a sanctuary when we consider its "efficiency and elegance in nature." Hollander's view on the suit is less to do with power or manipulation but more to do with comfort and grace.

Forms of Style

Amanda Brooks, the author of *I Love Your Style*, has classified style under the defined heads of Classic, Bohemian, Minimal, which could be complemented with undefinable style elements such as High Fashion, Street and Eclectic. As we progress our style palette we could get influenced by various accents and form a statement that is unique to us. These styles are not restricted to apparel and could bleed into other choices. Bohemian can be a lifestyle, from the food we eat, the books we read and the way we speak. It is important to go through an experimental phase before deciding on a style that suits us the best. Refraining from compartmentalizing within one box is important during an experimentation phase. Being able to cut through the clutter and carry what may travel and what may be edited is a skill that we can embrace through our life experience. As we evolve, so does our style.

Some boundaries have been crossed such as athletic wear combined with classic or something preppy and classic with bohemian. Pushing the boundaries on style offers vulnerability and an openness to embrace other forms and cultures. Brooks shares that her father would mix a Mexican tunic and Birkenstocks with chic, center-pleated khaki pants and a gold Rolex watch. Confidence is key to being able to pull off an eclectic mix between the classic/conventional and the bohemian/non-conventional. Ralph Waldo Emerson said, "Insist on yourself; never imitate." This precludes experimentation, which may be influenced by others. With our own style awakening, we can design an experience where everything comes together, reflective of our thoughts, our alliances and our form. It becomes more important than ever to remain conscious that trends are less important to our style than influences that may belong in any era or genre.

Awakening to our own style starts with self-awareness and initial experimentation followed by definition. If you have an intellectual vibe and like to read, you may draw up a list of role models and influencers you admire and decide to emulate some aspects of their personality, such as a particular style of pants or style of glasses, but you may wish to add eccentric socks that are your own signature or a certain color that is becoming of your skin and hair tone. Running the style by those who know you and an expert such as an image consultant can help you fine tune your own style and the way you wish to present yourself to the world.

Style Sourced from Nature

Frederick Fekkai, a celebrity hair designer and well known philosopher of style, shares that the "appreciation of nature teaches us to have style because it gives us a gentler, wiser and more poetic view of the world." I agree with Fekkai that some of the most stylish people are deeply influenced by nature. Not only does nature feed us colors and textures, it touches all our senses. If we can style ourselves through nature, we can exude a style that is never outdated or out of place. Nature greets us every morning as a fresh experience.

Our world is increasingly moving away from superficial power. There is greater emphasis on sustainability and life on the planet. This sentiment has come to permeate business purpose and finds expression in brands and influences the personal style of those who embrace such brands. A hybrid or electric vehicle, a Patagonia jacket,

Allbirds shoes, water from a can that says Liquid Death; the list is endless of businesses styling their brands to send a distinct message of sustainability and their closeness to nature. Embracing such brands influences our style as being conscious of our consumption and its impact on nature. Such a shift is unique and celebratory of our times. Designing a style statement that is close to nature is having a moment in history that is well-timed, as we allow nature to guide our style.

There is a natural grace and magnetism in animals and the stylish silhouette of trees, in addition to the daily theater of sunrise, sunset, the rain, the horizon, blue skies, leaves nodding in the breeze, and so much more. Nature can be an endless feeder for style, not just in appearance but in mood and manner if we train ourselves to listen for the unspoken and lead our response, guided by our senses, when we interact with others.

Some of the wealthiest people I know are interested in forestry, root systems, organic and regenerative farming, animals, and their natural habitat. The architecture of their homes are getting closer to natural materials and biophilic design, with its roots in nature. Such a foundation in nature can transport to everyday life in a rural or urban setting, in an office or at home. Style sourced from nature is a natural way to be stylish and build trust in relationships.

Self-Awareness and Style

When we design our style with nature in mind, it is important for us to have a clear understanding of who we are, as surmised by Socrates's philosophy of "know thyself." Our style must be authentic and natural to us. A style that is effortless, even as it may have an urbane, sophisticated air, is one that would be best to embrace. We must be driven at our core, by why we may be comfortable with our choice of a certain style. Affectations without authenticity are easily sniffed out, come off as shallow and worse still, fake. Instead of denying who we are, we can embrace our true selves to form a style that is real, with a signature that we can carry unapologetically as our own. Frederick Fekkai points out:

> You cannot force things to be what they aren't.
> From the way you smile to the way you walk,
> dress, eat or talk. Be authentic.
> Stay away from what's artificial.
> I know for a fact that,
> even more than so-called good taste,
> what you need to have is style that
> is nature inspired with an unpretentious way
> of looking at things.

I find such an outlook valuable because of its emphasis on self-awareness and nature. If we design our style to be close to our nature and to nature as a whole, we can be authentic, unapologetically ourselves and stylish. Not artificially, but effortlessly, like a gazelle.

> The confidence of yes
> The power of no
> The sense of adventure
> And the labor of love
> That is beautiful
> To be powerful and possible
> Fearless and vulnerable
> To be loving and loved
> Sometimes all at once
> That is beautiful ~ Frederick Fekkai

The ability to be possible and powerful, fearless and vulnerable, bears out our humanness and reflects an unpretentious style that is easy to relate to. I contacted Frederick Fekkai several years ago on a visit to New York. Given his celebrity status, I did not think I would be able to reach him easily and was prepared to speak to someone on his team. I was pleasantly surprised when he spoke with me directly and engaged at length on my aspirations, lifestyle and what may be suited to my style. The call was inconclusive as we would have needed to meet in person to come up with a signature style. The experience of connecting with him over a random call and his interest in me gifted me with the most pleasant experience. When I did meet him in person, some years later at his salon in Beverley Hills, the experience was better, yet. Fekkai embodies a style where engaging with him is informative and effortlessly pleasant. He is intuitive with his design and authentic despite his urbane sophistication.

Style and Aesthetics

A conversation on style would be incomplete without a reference to aesthetics. Of the many forms of beauty, Immanuel Kant's purposeless approach is the purest form of appreciation. When we admire a baby we experience beauty disinterested from purpose or utility, we experience simply the joy of seeing a beautiful baby, a pure unadulterated feeling. Kant's view of aesthetics is rooted in enjoying something for its own sake, without the corrupting forces of utility or purpose. Designing our style with self-awareness, inspired by nature, reflective of true interest in others, disengaged from purpose, can create an experience that is unintentionally stylish and influential.

Throughout my career I have advised professionals to look within themselves first, to "know thyself," before attempting to create a personal style. I now include, forget what you wish to achieve. Enjoy the experience, because if you like your style, you are more likely to be liked by others. Your choice of fashion is best if it is suited to you and drawn from the natural cycles of the world around you. Become more comfortable in cultivating a sense of style that is yours and yours alone, and witness how others become drawn to you.

FIVE

Incidentals

Manning Avenue, Los Angeles, is a stone's throw away from the high-rise office buildings of Century City. The area is a nice blend of residential and commercial neighborhoods. I could run my home office from a condo nestled unobtrusively in a three-storied building on Manning, and yet share the same zip code as the upscale office block on Wilshire Boulevard. It offered me the best of both worlds, a business address and a comfortable urbane dwelling.

The doorbell at my apartment rang on a Friday afternoon in the summer of 2012. I ushered in a small crew who were helping me with the production of a coffee table book, *Talent Through a New Lens*. The book was an introduction of our boutique firm to an upscale executive community. We were designing it to be spiffy, with excellent visuals on glossy art paper, complete with short, catchy messages in *Baskerville font*. The production team included a fine art photographer, we were sifting through his picture library from Paris, mainly the 16th arrondissement when I came upon an arresting image, taken from the top of Musée du Louvre. The image captured a panoramic view of the cobblestoned public square, *Place du Caroussel*, the shot captured the aerial view of the cobblestone masonry and a dwarfed imprint of a large black umbrella sheltering a young couple. It was hypnotic. "Why would you choose this image for a book styled for CEOs?" Vincent queried. "Because the view from the top is only any good if you can appreciate the beauty below," was my modest response. I looked at the image, over and over again, where were they going? They must be in love to share an umbrella, did they have a bag with produce for supper? Were they students? I was reminded of the old *Hollies* song:

> Bus stop, wet day
> She's there I say,
> Please share my umbrella
> Bus stops, bus goes
> She stays, love grows
> Under my umbrella

The text accompanying the image was a reminder of why the best leaders succeed when they can dismiss the ivory tower and admire the beauty below, the everyday people, sometimes invisible at the high altitude of success. My instincts on selecting this message to convey a leadership nugget was well received. The incidental image spoke of purpose, beauty, youthful liberty, love, shot in the midst of a light drizzle.

Everyone loved it for the emotions it stirred. Leadership involves service to those in our circle of care, and the circle can keep expanding with success. Ironically, an appreciation of beauty below the top is the only way to expand the circle and sustain success at the highest level.

We are conditioned to enjoy grand experiences that happen occasionally and ignore the inconvenient, banal occurrences that happen everyday. I never tire of citing David Foster Wallace's famous commencement speech at Kenyon College, *This is Water*. During the speech, he mentions the interaction between some fish. An older fish asks two younger fish, "Morning boys, how's the water?" The two young fish swim along for a while and then one of them looks at the other and says, "What the hell is water?" Wallace then riffs about standing in line in a grocery queue, and the many frustrations faced while waiting. When he decides to change his perspective from criticism and impatience towards understanding, enquiring, and caring, he begins to celebrate the experience of the quotidian. These incidental occurrences, in plain sight, are often overlooked by us.

Grand events and festivities are important experiences that we design with care, yet it is the challenging, boring and sometimes agonizing moments we confront and have to live with that become meaningful, even enjoyable when designed with intention.

Young and poor with a headful of dreams is a well known and laudable trope of aspiration. We are now encountering the reverse, a tidal wave of mid-career professionals, laid off and unable to find employment. A report from Bank of America indicated that in July 2025, Americans earning at least $125,000 a year were laid off at three times the rate of those with low or moderate incomes. There is a growing number of "functionally unemployed," seeking work and unable to find positions despite persistent efforts. Involuntary manager terminations have a 400% rise between January 2022 and September 2024, according to Gusto. For the first time in 45 years, individuals with a bachelor's degree or higher have a greater unemployment rate than the national average. Add to this the displacement created by AI, the chasm can be beyond income disparity, what we face is the brittle boundary between income and no income. The vortex from such displacement has many consequences. A study by WHO on social connection, states that 1 in 6 people worldwide is affected by loneliness, with significant impact on health and well being. Such a position can exacerbate when teamed with a lack of income. The basics of food, shelter, and possible healthcare may not be enough to tend to various issues that arise from unoccupied intelligence and a departure from pursuits that demand more than basic survival. The adjustment phase may involve finding solace and beauty in what I refer to as incidentals. My reference to incidentals in this context is the importance of the small things in life that are vital and just as critical to our existence as our pursuit of bigger goals.

In our rush to problem solve, we can get preoccupied with utilitarian priorities, creating budgets for non-existent income and pursuing traditional employment when the train for this may have already departed. A person with a mid-career derailment, or who may find themselves on a professional road less traveled, can be harder to place in traditional roles within companies. However, by tapping into our creativity and taking a peripheral view of the incidental, we can find new and fulfilling ways to pursue our calling. A transition towards creative solutions, entrepreneurship, hybrid arrangements that address our holistic needs—including the qualitative and the banal—call out the urgency to rescue the soul. This is just as vital as our rational, corporeal existence. To guide us through this valley of soul-searching, *Leaves of Grass* by Walt Whitman is a valuable companion (more so than a spreadsheet):

> We don't read and write poetry because it's
> cute. We read and write poetry because we
> are members of the human race.
> And the human race is filled with passion.
> So medicine, law, business, engineering,
> these are noble pursuits and necessary to
> sustain life. But poetry, beauty, romance,
> love. These are what we stay alive for.

Few would disagree that eating gourmet in New York City on a shoestring budget is impossible. I argue that it is possible, although my advice is colored heavily by my personal experience and may not be universally true. Living in New York, mid-career, as a student, following a business closure, was intellectually expansive yet financially constrained. I was accustomed to eating out at expensive restaurants and entertaining guests over elaborate sit-down dinners. A pure mathematical approach to the problem would have seen me eating lettuce, bread and soup from a can, possibly noodles and a rare chinese takeaway if I was feeling generous. But *Oliver asked for more*. Why is it that a greasy biscuit with bacon and eggs costs less than a cup of steamed spinach? And why do the many mom and pop shops in Bushwick not offer steamed spinach in the first place? Why is the option to eat healthy restricted to expensive bistros?

Stewing in negativity or adjusting my food habits to the limitations of my wallet were both uninspiring solutions. Shopping at big box retail stores yielded family-sized packs, when fresh produce was my craving. Farmer's Markets were unaffordable. Happenstance, I found a couple of ethnic stores that would pile their produce from the inner shelves onto outer tables once a week. This clearance at discounted rates created room for fresh produce inside. On such days, you could buy artichoke, arugula, turnips, bits of salmon and many of my favorites, at a fraction of the regular price, sometimes at one dollar for a batch and in much better condition than eating frozen food. I could fix myself a king's salad with a drizzle of balsamic and olive oil within a five dollar spend. Likewise, I learned that at the stroke of 8 pm, a few grocers near Union Square knocked off fifty percent from their regular price for prepared foods; what is not consumed becomes garbage. The offer is limited to less than an hour before closing time. Despite these discoveries, I would treat myself to a really fancy smoked salmon and capers on a bagel with gourmet coffee at a favorite bistro, once a week, and settle for plain toast on other days to cover the deficit. This was not so much about an orgy with food but a way to restore my spirit by learning to savor the incidentals while not losing touch with gourmet experiences.

Keeping up with cultural pursuits was less challenging with the many libraries, and art exhibitions held in New York, yet theater is never cheap in the city. Unlike the Geffen in LA, where rush tickets are easy to secure, Broadway was harder to navigate. I learned to enjoy the theater at the *grand magasins* on fifth avenue, window shopping and enjoying the ambience at the Bergdorf Goodman, where once I could shop with the abandon of a drunken sailor. It would've been harder to adjust to the changed status if I had kept to the old lens without adjusting to a new vision, grounded in purpose. I became interested in the lives of the frontline staff, noticing the livery of the doorman, understanding the store design and the connection to the display. There were fresh insights that would not have surfaced in my consciousness without what Neil Gaiman calls, "a view from the cheap seats." The distance to the banal, particularly when the special was *de rigueur,* can only be crossed by leaning into our creativity and inner banks of literature. For me, it was a way to rescue my soul.

The Spirit of Smiley

In the world of art, the Smiley Face designed by Harvey Ball is possibly the most popular and incidental of art examples. The image pleased the world with the stroke of a pen. The returns for the simple design are unstoppable. This piece of art gained in value similar to a Picasso or a Matisse. The image is pure, uncomplicated and never fails to bring a smile to the beholder. A less known fact is Harvey Ball's reaction to what many may consider, "being cheated out of the returns."Harvey was busy solving client problems. When the State Mutual Life Assurance Company gave him an assignment to improve employee morale with a mission to make them smile, Ball created the Smiley Face in a flash of inspiration. He got the dimensions just right, distinguishing Smiley from other happy faces. Smiley is hugely expressive. The popularity for the Smiley Face soared to over 50 million orders, although Harvey Ball was only compensated $45 as the original fee for his design. Ball's genius was unprotected by copyright. When he contacted attorneys, he was told that the Smiley Face was now in the public domain and an international icon, it was too late to award him any more than what he had earned originally. Ball walked away graciously and embodied the spirit of his artwork, instead of putting up a fight. He designed a charity titled *World Smile Foundation,* promoting children's causes. He moved the lens away from resentment and redirected it towards spreading happiness.

This may appear naive and unworldly in today's context, yet when you consider his position, he may have acted appropriately. As a small business tasked to do a very small job, the explosive success was totally unprecedented. Had he made a big deal at the outset, he may have run the risk of losing the client's interest. He got the job done. The bigger question involves the insurance company and subsequent owners such as Franklin Loufrani, who extensively licensed Smiley, or Bernard and Murray Spain who trademarked a version of Smiley Face with the message "Have a Nice Day." Could any of them have included Ball in the rewards of the ensuing success? They did not have to do so and they did not.

It can be hard to open such conversations retroactively and it remains a mystery whether there could have been a way to reward Ball in any other befitting manner. Today, the Smiley Company's revenues are $500 million annually, whereas the original architect of the design earned no more than $45. The contrast is glaring and stands out as a missed opportunity for what could have been a happier progression. The main takeaway for me was that Ball acted wisely, he rejoiced in the success of his craft and directed his energies towards greater fulfilment. Purpose can bring clarity and center us on what matters the most, and in doing so can shield us from distractions and the dissipation of our energy. Bringing a scorn to Smiley may have hurt his persona more than celebrating its success. He secured his place as the architect of what made the world happy and his legacy is irrevocable. John Masefield professed that the days that make us happy make us wise. We have an obligation to pursue happiness wholeheartedly to lead a fulfilled life. Harvey Ball was wise and exemplified this spirit.

Learning from Both Worlds

The late Chairman of Samsung Group, Lee Kun-hee famously said that it is difficult to scale back from luxuries once you get accustomed to them. This belief caused him to discourage his team from flying first class and he deprived himself from several luxuries that may have been within his grasp. I would respect and challenge his position. Not being over indulgent and wasteful of expenses is worthy of respect, yet experiencing luxury to learn and expand awareness while being comfortable with the banal, is nirvana. The ultimate emancipation, made possible when we learn to celebrate the ordinary. Such celebration need not be at the cost of depriving ourselves of a grand experience, which may actually be enhanced by experiencing both sides. YSL was celebrated in Paris for his unique Moroccan influence, not so much for his knowledge of Paris, he could blend both worlds for a distinctly refreshing experience. Awareness helps us upgrade everyday experiences if we fuel our actions with purpose.

The life of a struggling entrepreneur can easily become isolated and minimalist. My business closure led me into a corner. I was accustomed to conversing with CEOs and well known personalities who had been instrumental in enabling my own development. My community of colleagues, clients and friendships changed as my professional life took an entrepreneurial turn that led to a business closure. I was put on pause till I became successful again and to my dismay, I was struck off the A-list. I received support through formal, regulated, often rationed communication. Such social isolation was not an enviable position. Yet I grew in other ways, I learned to make small talk with bartenders and kept up with my innate love of hair stylists, jewelry designers, florists, tailors and shoemakers. While I could still afford the occasional drink at a favored bar, I met the rest for an occasional hello, when in town, as their former customer. I grew from experiencing another world and had more to offer my few well-placed relationships that had journeyed with me through the rough and tumble. I had gathered deep insights at the bottom that I could never have experienced in my previous, well-compensated job.

If we can travel the diverse roads we may need to take with consciousness, the luxurious and the incidental find a balance. Although inconvenienced and somewhat saddened by the change, I could keep my spirit from waning because I could understand both perspectives. I had faith that I would find my place again if I stayed true to my work and my priorities. Partaking of an expensive glass of wine when possible and an iced lemonade on other days are both enjoyable and worthy of our indulgence.

Almost every wise person encourages us to reduce and eliminate as there is more to be gained by subtracting and simplifying than by adding. Who in their right senses enjoys clutter? Not even those who create it. My view of this perception supports making the right additions. We eliminate the clutter and create room for preferred pursuits and acquisitions. Elimination without addition may lead us to a void, an emptiness if we do not replace and add what may be worth embracing. We can enhance our list of favorite things while continuing to eliminate unfavorable items. Expanding and contracting are symbiotic by their very nature when placed on the axis of consciousness. Not predisposed to collecting junk, I did find joy in my engagement with a few artifacts and vintage furniture that I possessed. Certain objects have life.

Some Objects Have Life

The concept of animism is based on the belief that all material phenomena have agency. The anthropologist Edward Tylor described it as a common practice with many Indigenous peoples. My interpretation of animism is not a sweeping acceptance of all objects, but a few that hold special meaning. The connection with such objects is not motivated by fetish as much as a memory-link between the tactile and the spatial. They become placeholders and memory markers, stirring our senses when we re-engage with them. A few objects of such significance were stored away by me as I navigated a lengthy, professional crossing. When reunited with these special belongings I felt a similar rush as when I greeted an old friend. They stirred my senses beyond the obvious ones of touch, smell and sight—they opened floodgates of memory inlaid in good design. You do not have to be a synesthete to know that perfumes, colors, and sounds echo one another, as Baudelaire so beautifully stated.

Eliminating and preserving can be difficult when necessity demands such change. The journey from a Ming vase to a crystal one was difficult for me until I could reappropriate my taste by injecting my love of roses. Roses look beautiful in a crystal vase and would be out of place in a Ming ornament. The incidental joy of common flowers in a crystal vase facilitated the expansion of good taste. The re-assembly allowed me to celebrate the ordinary without unduly bemoaning the loss of the expensive. We can expand our repertoire with everyday objects without any loss of good taste by adding easy activities such as sending handwritten, vintage postcards to our friends. It does not cost much and, if well-composed, such memorabilia are seldom thrown away.

A Culture Walk

One of my memorable incidental experiences is a walk with a colleague in Singapore's Chinatown. When I lived in Singapore, I would sometimes visit Chinatown to escape the expatriate ghetto of Holland Village, my neighborhood. The sounds, smells, and colors of Chinatown weave a certain magic, not easily found in other quarters. On one such visit with a colleague who is a Sinophile, I discovered Chinatown in new ways. My colleague would stop by a casement and explain why it was painted a certain green, the bright green's generative significance and link to paddy fields. I could visualize the five elements of wood, fire, earth, metal, and water in a playground where alleyways met architecture. My high-level understanding of Feng Shui sunk in. I love working with chinoiserie, particularly when it intersects with Parisian style. We exchanged notes on how a touch of chinoiserie can make a pocket-size *pied à terre* feel sumptuous and elegant. I learned that *yuan-yi* was the Chinese name for the horseshoe chair with its message of symmetry and unity. The rendezvous that had effortlessly turned into a culture walk came to an end as we walked up Trengganu Street to Yum Cha, a dim sum restaurant. We ordered a few batches of dim sum and a pot of jasmine tea. The conversation moved to the office, the upcoming offsite in Shanghai and some colorful, harmless gossip. My subsequent visits to Chinatown were never the same. I grew from the experience and now understood the essence of Chinatown in a deeper way.

Designed Experiences Have a Longer Life

The allegory of the *Little Prince* is profoundly soulful. I never tire of its reference. Our small actions everyday can become uplifting when we commiserate with literature. I share here a few excerpts from Antoine de Saint-Exupéry's

The Little Prince, that I have found to be eternally relevant:

> "I am looking for friends. What does that mean--tame?"
> "It is an act too often neglected," said the fox. It means to establish ties."
> "To establish ties'?" "Just that," said the fox.
> "To me, you are still nothing more than a little boy who is just like a hundred thousand other little boys. And I have no need of you.
> And you, on your part, have no need of me.
> To you, I am nothing more than a fox like a hundred thousand other foxes.
> But if you tame me, then we shall need each other.
> To me, you will be unique in all the world.
> To you, I shall be unique in all the world."

The experience lends us unique insights, distinguished from superficial interactions. The fox and the prince became special to one another, by taming each other, their relationship grew:

> "My life is very monotonous," the fox said. "I hunt chickens; men hunt me. All the chickens are just alike, and all the men are just alike. And, in consequence, I am a little bored. But if you tame me, it will be as if the sun came to shine on my life. I shall know the sound of a step that will be different from all the others.
> Other steps send me hurrying back underneath the ground. Yours will call me, like music, out of my burrow. And then look: you see the grain-fields down yonder? I do not eat bread. Wheat is of no use to me. The wheat fields have nothing to say to me. And that is sad. But you have hair that is the color of gold. Think how wonderful that will be when you have tamed me! The grain, which is also golden, will bring me back the thought of you. And I shall love to listen to the wind in the wheat."

Someone wisely said, you can live a moment thrice, in anticipation, in reality, and in memory. Whenever possible, I prefer a planned meeting where the experience can have an extended life. By designing the experience, we extend its life. The resonance with the passages below offers a glance into finding shards of joy even as death may stalk us at the edges:

> "It would have been better to come back at the same hour," said the fox. "If, for example, you come at four o'clock in the afternoon, then at three o'clock I shall begin to be happy. I shall feel happier and happier as the hour advances. At four o'clock, I shall already be worrying and jumping about. I shall show you how happy I am. But if you come at just any time, I shall never know at what hour my heart is to be ready to greet you."

The fox continues his commentary on the significance of a planned interlude:

> "There is a rite, for example, among my hunters. Every Thursday they dance with the village girls. So Thursday is a wonderful day for me, I can take a walk as far as the vineyards. But if the hunters danced at just any time, every day would be like every other day, and I should never have any vacation at all."

Designing an experience for incidental, day-to-day occurrences involves thoughtfulness and a desire to preserve pleasant moments in memory. Proust's association with a simple madeleine cake dipped in a cup of tea evoked memories that filled pages of his seminal work, *In Search of Lost Time*. An incidental remembrance can open the floodgates of memory.

By readjusting my view from the top to see the beauty below, I came to understand that there are many small, precious moments that we can miss in plain sight. In paying attention to such moments, I realized I could always hold a positive attitude. I now hold onto my art books, influential paperbacks, handwritten notes, and other art and mementos—rich symbols of incidental experiences, which I've learned are often worth more than any impersonal, grand affair.

SIX

Luxury

Influential names in the luxury industry such as Karl Lagerfeld, Celine, Loro Piana, Tom Ford, Marcel Wanders and many others have advocated a nuanced view for the term "luxury," not one synonymous with a high price tag, or status symbol only, where the buyer assumes that expensive items offer a badge of success. Good luxury brands would rather be known for timelessness, style, a mindset that creates space for ease and expression, quality craftsmanship, and increasingly, sustainable production and sourcing methods that justify the high price tag. A T-Shirt in a Chanel suit or an expensive watch worn with blue jeans, epitomize the ease and acceptance for something expensive in everyday life; the contrast of aspiration blended with the ordinary, sends a message of sophistication and gains a nod of approval from taste-makers. By contrast, someone dressed entirely in flashy expensive clothes and accessories may come off as lacking in good taste, even if the price tag screams out as being expensive.

My relationship with the luxury industry began with crafting holidays, travel and retreats comprising special experiences. As my career progressed, I served a cadre of brands in the luxury goods and services sector. The classic tension between product and experience is an ongoing debate in the industry. Those that sell experiences, such as luxury travel, hotels and fine dining, go to great lengths to try and make the experience tangible, whereas luxury goods companies try and engage customers through experiences and stories to enliven the product. The weavers of experiences or makers of products both try to deliver a tune that strikes the right chord for a premium price tag.

Chip Conley, the Founder of Joie de Vivre Hospitality, known for his contemporary thinking, raised an important question at a fireside chat. "What would a 7 star hotel be?" Even the most expensive hotel suite at $100,000 per night ends at a 5 star, the *Atlantis The Royal* in Dubai. Would it then be a place that serves the diamond shaped Glorious Bonbon, the most expensive chocolate created by chocolatier Daniel Gomes, for over $9000? Of course not. There is a limit to how far a price tag or rating can go, and if indeed a fantasy place of 7 stars were to exist, it would likely be famous for the way we experience the service; possibly for the comfort and calm it brings us or a memory that we would cherish forever. Most discerning buyers and sellers of luxury products and services give emotional connection as much weight as the exclusivity they offer.

Pauline Brown, a longtime leader in the luxury goods industry and pioneer in the business of aesthetics, defines aesthetics as a perception of the senses, how objects and experiences make us feel. Brown suggests that attunement between self-awareness and the sensory translate into deeper and often pleasurable feelings in an aesthetic experience. Such consciousness can allow us to touch others with heightened aesthetic awareness, making our interactions more pleasurable and sensuous.

Studying Design

As a student pursuing graduate studies at Parsons School of Design in New York, I could study the psyche and lives of designers through the intimacy of their craft. Design is foundational to the luxury industry and the basis for a premium product or service. An evening gown by Schiaparelli, a designer painstakingly resurrected by the genius of Creative Director, Daniel Roseberry, can cost as much as $17,000. It is over fifty years since Elsa Schiaparelli's passing, yet her innovation and design philosophy have endured. I became deeply influenced by Schiaparelli, not only for her designs but also for her approach to life. She was an untrained designer, who did not rise through the ranks of *arpette, second main* and *premiere main*, yet she could enter at the top and earn the patronage of Paris's café society. As an Italian couturier her success was not achieved in her native Italy, but in France. In her biography *Shocking Life,* she shares that in France she felt like "a very favored stepchild." Such acceptance was possible because of her innovative style—she drew inspiration from everywhere, body parts, lobsters and tears as motifs on dresses, a shoe as a hat. Despite such craziness, she could be refined, her greatest fans were ultra-smart and conservative women, wives of diplomats, bankers, millionaires and artists. The paradox of chaos and calmness found acceptance with some of the most traditional clientele. Her first big break came from Lord and Taylor in New York, when they ordered 40 copies of the famous black sweater with a white trompe l'oeil bow.

Although her genius was behind one of the world's best couture brands, her struggles along the way are less known. She sometimes had to sustain herself on small portions of fruit and an occasional serving of meat, from stalls frequented by bus drivers and workers. Her memoirs reinforce a strict code from her righteous, aristocratic roots that inhibited her from succumbing to dubious choices, or compromising on quality; she took the right path even when it was a difficult one. Schiaparelli's lifestyle was often rocked by hardship, as a single parent and a struggling entrepreneur.

The playfulness of her designs in the interwar period, so loved by a discerning clientele, are marked by humor and surrealism, as is her personal life. A conversation—

in which she reassured her daughter Gogo as she queried about the graves of Napoleon and his aides at a cemetery in Paris—turned into a salutation in their personal letters. Schiaparelli shares in her memoirs,"we often end our letters, Napoleon and all his little soldiers," as a mark of love and solidarity, instead of the standard hugs and kisses. In another situation, when she was forced to live in a mouse-ridden apartment, she could find humor. "I got a small fox terrier, hoping he would keep the rats away, but he was even more terrified than me, at the first sound of a mouse, he crawled into my bed. We had to get up in the small hours of the morning, the courageous dog and I, to go to a nearby hotel and get some sleep." At the center of Schiaparelli's design is her innovation, playfulness and philosophy; she brought her life and soul to her work, making her a legend in her lifetime.

In the Midst of Winter

Some years are colder than others in New York, but invariably January and February are the coldest months. I visited New York frequently during 2016 and moved there permanently for the following two years. I lived one street over from the novelist Isabel Allende's apartment, where she had written *In The Midst of Winter,* while snowbound in Brooklyn. Who knows, we may have passed each other at the neighborhood cafe, incognito in dark coats and winter scarves. Unlike the time I had met her at a book signing event in Mill Valley's independent store, *Book Passage,* on a spring afternoon in northern California.

January of 2018 saw another major winter storm, a blizzard called the *bomb cyclone.* By February, the snowfalls were lighter but the air, biting cold. A light drizzle turned the snow into icicle bridges on windowpanes.

Peter Høeg's book *Smilla's Sense of Snow* takes us on a journey of the Inuit and the myriad ways in which they experience snow. Unlike the commonly used terms of sleet and snow, the Inuit experience snow with an array of characteristics: *Qanik* stands for big, weightless crystals that fall in clumps; *Pirhuk* means light, wind-blown snow; *Apuhiniq,* drifted snow, and there are several other variations that make up a long list. *Pirhirhuq* refers to the type of weather that produces a snowstorm. That February saw us recovering from a *Pirhirhuq.*

I had arrived at Dover Street Market, run by Japanese fashion label Comme des Garçons, in Midtown Manhattan. I was walking the streets of Chelsea, flâneur-like in my study of the designer Rei Kawakubo. Aware of her activism from exhibits such as *Lumps and Bumps,* held at MoMA, and Andrew Bolton's curation of *Art of the In-between* at the Met, I knew of Rei Kawakubo as the post-modernist designer known for her experimental use of scale, color, symbolism, and pop culture. Rei has been the subject of a longstanding debate between art and fashion, relating audiences and buyers to apparel as an artist would to their art. Kawakubo's design has been criticized as an assault on fashion. She has drawn inspiration from rags and stitches that emulate social conditions such as homelessness. Despite such radical creativity, she has secured a spot in haute couture. Her palette can mimic Charles Baudelaire's *Ragpicker's Wine:*

> In the muddy maze of some old neighborhood,
> Often, where the street lamp gleams like blood,
> As the wind whips the flame, rattles the glass,
> Where human beings ferment in a stormy mass,
>
> One sees a ragpicker knocking against the walls,
> Paying no heed to the spies of the cops, his thralls,
> But stumbling like a poet lost in dreams;
> He pours his heart out in stupendous schemes
> ~Charles Baudelaire

Kawakubo's eccentricity finds a master-nose expression in her perfume creations that capture out of the ordinary city smells, such as *Tar and Dry Clean*.

The Dover Street Market store has an unexpected location, close to Curry Hill, instead of being predictably located in the fashion district. It is housed in a culturally rich, circa 1908 building with classical frieze. Designed by architect Harvey Wiley Corbett, the facility was a former art institute for women. Arriving at the building, one is met by a sense of calm, offering no clue to the chaos inside. The innards of the store drew me into a busy bazaar experience, part museum display and part merchandise, housed in seven floors of mismatch and discordance. The spaces did not bleed into each another, instead they represented broken, disparate architecture, where Prada and skateboarder conflicted. Giant, colorful, knitted columns created sartorial fantasy, as the basement mimicked a do-it-yourself store. The visitors, a combination of locals and tourists along with the store hands, blended perfectly in this luxury retail theater.

Comme des Garçons' Dover Street Market space was suspended between design and fashion, aesthetics and architecture where display mannequins and racks had as much personality as the clothes they carried. A world of interruptions and interpretations that expressed the designer's innovative style. Yet there was unity and cohesiveness in the disruption and unpredictability. It was surprising to find other big name designers such as Gucci and Prada sharing Kawakubo's shopfloor in an industry known for arch rivalry. The team spirit and collaboration were telling of Kawakubo's ability to mobilize the collective. Dover Street Market comes across as a hipster store, described by Chris Bagley of Bloomberg' in an article titled *Behind Comme des Garçons is Zen-Loving Contrarian*, as a "multi brand Mecca, part fashion emporium, part group art installation, and part, Peewee's Playhouse." Under such originality lay a successful business, evoking collaboration more than competition.

Rei Kawakubo's avant-garde vintage designs can fetch as much as $32,000 and her furniture designs can be auctioned for close to $28,000. Kawakubo offers a unique and refreshing twist to the luxury fashion experience in complete contrast with industry norm.

Subversive Techniques

Kawakubo's subversive techniques find a kindred spirit in Martin Margiela. Margiela is known for his creativity and enquiring spirit. He has held positions at Jean Paul Gaultier and Hermes, has led his own fashion house, Maison Martin Margiela, and grown it into a public company. Some of Margiela's radical concepts have found an early voice in the *Exhibition 9/4/1615* held at Museum Boijmans Van Beuningen in Rotterdam, where detritus and decay came together in a microbe heavy, poetic installation. Eighteen garments, saturated in mold, created an intriguing visual, like garden husks, alive, ghostlike, flapping in the wind against the glass doors of the museum that opened towards the garden. The mold and bacteria let the mute figures speak, as melancholy ghosts, creating a *coup de theatre*, visually breathtaking and intellectually provocative. Instead of catwalks, Margiela is known to hold his shows in derelict spaces such as parks, wasteland and warehouses, approximating fine art installations and theatrical performance. Margiela's artistic predisposition in design has proven to be commercially successful with some of his vintage wear fetching as much as upwards of $100,000 at auction.

Designers like Ralph Lauren have proven that multi products and services can come together to form a cohesive experience where couture, sports, home decor, and restaurants can be experienced through the lens of lifestyle, like the sport of polo, without being a literal connection to polo sportsgear or equipment. Polo expresses a nuance where a vibe can tie a product range and be experienced intimately, creating loyalty despite the disparity. The lifestyle of Ralph Lauren products tell a timeless story, bringing luxury within reach, through ready to wear garments, yet keeping a distance from fast fashion, aspirational and exclusive within the club-like preppy fantasy of Polo. It is also an everyday, all-American choice for sportswear, as celebrated by American athletes at the Paris Olympics, 2024. Ralph Lauren exemplifies having his cake and eating it too by weaving an alluring myth with Polo—he is within reach, and yet, exclusive.

The Changing Face of Luxury

The changing face of luxury goods is expected to gain more ground through inclusivity than exclusivity. We see this shift with long standing traditional players like Tiffany and Company and their tutelage of a new breed of designers like multi-hyphenate Pharrell Williams. His rebellious creativity, expressed through bold designs, helps penetrate new grounds and demographics for Tiffany.

The luxury industry faces the ongoing challenge of maintaining its exclusive edge while expanding market share and being perceived as a responsible, planet friendly and socially conscious business. At a grassroots level this can be seen in the ongoing gentrification and cultural renaissance in working class neighborhoods. Plays like *A Bronx Tale* are aimed at building awareness and fostering the development of neighborhoods like The Bronx. At a broader level we see a greater commitment to the planet and sustainability. The apparel industry has historically been the second biggest pollutant, next only to oil and gas. With rising public awareness, there is greater pressure in the luxury industry to become more transparent and democratic with their inner workings while keeping to an upscale position. The convergence of the classic with the contemporary forces a greater emphasis on inclusivity.

Commercial pressures force engagement with newer, younger demographics, while keeping the classic experience well-designed for legacy clientele. Diversification through accessories that bring entry points within reach without destroying the signature brands that continue to maintain a high price tag is a strategic move by almost all luxury goods and services today.

Second Hand Retail

The rising popularity of second hand retail is another major leap towards inclusivity and presents a challenge for traditional luxury businesses. A vintage piece of jewelry purchased through any reputed ecommerce platform is at a fraction of what it costs first hand from the same brand's retail showroom. Once worn, it is impossible to tell whether it was bought first-or-second-hand. This is true of most luxury goods across all product segments. Companies like Rent the Runway add to the pressure by diverting customers away from traditional shopping, bringing luxury items within reach of everyday consumers at very affordable price points. Within this dynamic landscape, the experience becomes even more important. Through experience and common purpose, consumers move from acquisition to an emotional bond. They feel enlisted and wish to see their darling brand survive and succeed. A deeply felt experience is vital in moving the connection from a transaction to a loyal relationship.

There is an increasing desire amongst the discerning and self-aware, to embrace the ordinary within the extraordinary, making the quotidian fashionable, this phenomenon is sometimes referred to as the *prole drift*. The DHL polo shirt by Vetements is an example where an industrial, everyday uniform finds a place in premium retail. The self-taught textiles practitioner Tom van Deijnen has promoted a positive movement in clothing repairs, darning and mending as a social and cultural activity. The concept draws from arts and crafts movements and presents a responsible form of social activism in apparel. Beautiful, obviously visible mending on expensive apparel looks cool, likewise reimagined accessories promote design and creativity. An appreciation for design becomes a stepping stone for respect. We desire products and services that inspire us by their design.

Such initiatives create opportunities for events, workshops and community engagement. The luxury industry benefits from such embodied materialism, where values and design come together to form community involvement and conscious consumption. The business of luxury hangs on a precipice, where *plutôt la vie,* or "choose life," becomes an imperative with sustainability at its core. The Native American saying, "We do not inherit the earth from our ancestors; we borrow it from our children," holds truer than ever today. It offers a bridge for such goods and services to engage with conscious materialism where the total experience outshines a single transaction or purchase.

The concept of avant-gardism has gone through many iterations, sometimes described as newness, making it an attractive choice in contemporary design. Robert Hughes, the Australian art critic and writer, described avant-garde as "shock of the new." The term can oscillate between bohemianism and new thinking. The role of deconstruction and assembly form part of an avant-garde mindset. We are forced to re-examine the luxury industry for present day priorities. While the composer, Richard Wagner's illusionary "noble death" in favor of the collective or greater good is by no means an option for sellers or buyers, yet an intervention of healthy avant-gardism, as demonstrated by a series of designers, (all very successful commercially, despite pushing boundaries), creates openings for broadening the luxury experience. More touch points, education and improved communities, may result in no loss of exclusivity. On the contrary, it may bring added prestige that comes from pursuing a greater purpose.

SEVEN

Loss

I was at an eatery downstairs in Penn Station, amid commuters on a particularly busy evening as I waited for a train to Lancaster, Pennsylvania. I was staying in deep Amish country and commuting to New York for meetings. My visits to New York, from California, over the past two years had been close to the holidays, when the Big Apple transforms as a bejeweled Grand Dame, resplendent and dressed to the nines. I had taken a walk to the Bergdorf Goodman to view the festive windows that afternoon. The theme for 2024 was *Toast of the Town,* celebrating Fifth Avenue's 200th anniversary. A homage to cultural icons like the yellow cab sat alongside high fashion apparel sold inside the store, forming a batik of sensory colors, like a mood board for the year ahead.

For the first time, despite several prior visits, I had taken the time to learn about the Beaux-Arts influenced design of Penn Station. As a lifelong student of design, my favorite period is the 1920s and 30s. The United States celebrates this chapter of history the best, in my opinion. My design playbook is mainly colored by the cities I have lived in, Los Angeles and New York. I know of gems strewn across the country—Frank Lloyd Wright, David Adler, Paul Williams. These designers have left their stamp everywhere in the form of "exquisite corpses," Michael Sorkin's sardonic tag for beautiful, old urban buildings.

I thought there was no writer like Graham Greene until I discovered E.B. White. White's essay, *Here is New York,* considered a love letter to the city, resides in my memory as a cultural roadmap:

There are roughly three New Yorks. There is, first, the New York of the man or woman who was born here, who takes the city for granted and accepts its size and its turbulence as natural and inevitable. Second, there is the New York of the commuter — the city that is devoured by locusts each day and spat out each night. Third, there is the New York of the person who was born somewhere else and came to New York in quest of something.... Commuters give the city its tidal restlessness; natives give it solidity and continuity; but the settlers give it passion.

I was a commuter that day but not a regular locust as described by White. I was commuting as a visitor. Previously, I did come to the city on a quest, as a wannabe settler full of passion but my long history in California was hard to shed. I often feel lost between two shores, constantly re-establishing my moorings.

It was late evening and my train was arriving soon. Halfway to my destination on the train, I reached for my phone and it was nowhere. I looked and looked and could not find it. I asked a fellow passenger if I could use her phone to call my phone, in the hopes that someone would answer the call and tell me where it lay lost. I heard my familiar greeting on the voicemail but no answer. I had switched trains in Philadelphia and may have left it on the seat of the last train. I felt crushed, as if a yellow cab had run over me. The inconvenience of a lost phone was excruciating. It feels as though our life runs through our phones. I decided to take the train back to New York on the next stop, to see if I may have left my phone at the eatery, but alas, they did not have it. I filed a lost item report with Amtrak, and they said they would let me know within seventy-two hours if someone dropped the phone at the lost and found. My world was in shambles. Somehow I found my way on the last train back to Lancaster. I contacted Apple support from a different phone the next day.

A friendly and articulate voice greeted me: "not to worry, we will find your phone for you." I felt reassured and calm. I was gently guided on my Mac, which was con-nected to the phone, and I allowed the voice on the phone to share my screen. This was poetry in motion. The kindly customer support representative pulled up a map on my screen and could trace my lost phone to a coffee kiosk in Penn Station. He then disabled my phone securing all data and added a message on the screen to say that this was a lost phone and he included a number where I could be reached. All done remotely from my Mac. I had not slept the night before and collapsed in an exhausted stupor from relief. I called my lost phone when I woke up and a barista at the small coffee kiosk, where I had picked up a coffee for the road, answered. She said she would hold my phone for a week. She shared a note for everyone at the kiosk to say that I would be returning to fetch the phone.

My respect for Apple support was sky high. I experienced what good design, high tech and a human touch can do. This was the model everyone should emulate. On prior calls with Apple support, I have experienced a similar pleasant interface, although they were routine visits by comparison to the catastrophe I had just encountered. I collected my phone from the cafe kiosk the next day. Penn Station is among the busiest stations in the US, yet this little kiosk, with no pretense of good service, had painstakingly stowed my phone and handed it to me most graciously. Service at its best with a smile. Apple's customer support gave me peace of mind and the barista opened my eyes to New York's caring spirit. Whoever said leave New York before it makes you hard had not visited this little kiosk in Penn Station.

In the ocean of apps and bots offering instant chat support, help centers inviting a complaint and offering a ticket via AI with fictitious names for bots, Apple stands out as a breath of fresh air. Not only do they have the best technology, they pair it with a hospitable and efficient service, delivered by humans. This is an experience worth celebrating.

Time

My losses far exceed a temporary separation from my phone. There are some losses that are irrecoverable, like the passing of loved ones. I believe that material losses are recoverable. The lament for lost time is a more complicated matter—it is a leitmotif that we encounter every few years as we take stock of our goals, the risks we may have taken, rewards and unforeseen obstacles along the way. Sometimes we can gain time, by taking a step back. I have successfully intercepted periods of loss with measures that counter and uplift from the loss. Like going back to school after the closure of my last business. It was an antidote that brought fresh energy and learning. The investment could eventually save me time, possibly reverse misfortune by opening opportunities that bring good fortune and a more aligned pathway forward.

Loss of time, like life itself, is inevitable. We will lose time, even when it is well-spent. The secret may lie in adjusting time with our priorities, things that really matter to us and the time we have to achieve them. Missing a boat in life and chasing after it can quadruple the loss. If someone thinks they would have made a good lawyer and realize this at forty, perhaps pursuing law school may be a boat they missed, but the critical thinking about their vocation may prove fruitful in other ways. Self-awareness and pitching for what is best within the time and context at hand, ultimately saves us time. Regressing towards something that is a mismatch can add cumulative losses to the downward spiral of lost time, whereas situating ourselves where our skills can be put to good use extends our time.

I can relate well to Zadie Smith's point of view in *Killing Orson Welles at Midnight*—the same duration of time can mean different things at different times:

> You sit in the dark, trying to figure out *la règle du jeu*. Clearly there are two types of time, real and staged. There are a few ways to say that. Accidental clocks versus deliberate clocks. Time that has been caught on film versus time that has been manipulated for film. It turns out that accidental clocks are more poignant than deliberate clocks. The actors in the street valiantly approximate reality, but the clock tower behind them has captured reality, a genuine moment in time, now passed forever, unrecoverable, yet reanimated by film.

She adds:

> Between four and five o'clock transport is significant: trains, cars, and airplanes. If the phone rings after one in the morning do not expect good news. Cuckoo clocks, no matter when they chime, are almost always ominous. When Orson Welles says what time it is, it lends the hour an epic sound. At two AM everyone is lonely.

How do you set aside the loss from a business closure where you may have invested deeply? If it offers learning and can be a trophy for time well spent, then the same time has a different significance. A way forward to carry into a new space or to revisit and possibly realign. Sunk costs are only wasted when they are unaccounted for, doing things you may dislike or whiling away time without purpose. You remember nothing, the days get consumed, the money may be insignificant, it all may go up in a blue smoke.

Taking a dimensional view of lost time and money brings awareness and allows us to focus on where we may be best suited to recover from the loss in enduring and meaningful ways. How we experience time allows us to design for the ways we consume it, and thus, get more out of it, whether that's in a material sense or in the development of greater meaning and the time we spend finding such meaning.

Design and Life

In mid-2008, my father was given two months to live. He had all the care in the world but was on a downward spiral, depressed from the loss of my mother and brother. Unrecognizable, frail, he barely remembered me. He had day and night care plus a doctor on call, but he had lost his will to live. Only a miracle could make things better. Such trials test our mental agility, the problem before me needed surgical precision.

Our rambling old suburban home was in shambles, depressive and melancholy. I could only take two weeks away from work and somehow eked out another ten days. With the help of an excellent realtor, we sold our old house at a loss and bought a very pleasant small, luxury apartment which I redesigned with our old period furniture, refurbished. All things precious were reappointed, the same entourage of our family doctor and caregivers were transferred to the new abode. My father lived on for about six years, well beyond the prognosis of two months. The same care with new design, gave him a new lease on life. The financial loss from selling our home in a rush turned out to be a gain. We could extend life in a better habitat. A holistic view of time, money and loss sharpens our vision—we can ultimately gain from what may be perceived as a short-term loss and setback.

William Green, the author of *Richer, Wiser, Happier* speaks at length about investing by taking a holistic view where material gain is only as good as its ability to make us happier and wiser, not an end in itself. After acute losses, investors who have to start from scratch or those who may have lost their homes and belongings to a fire or any other form of *force majeure* can recover by centering themselves with core skills, prioritizing what matters most and removing the rest. Green suggests that we need to construct our bridge thoughtfully with "friends along the path" who can help us to reconnect, rejuvenate and recover.

Back on Boogie Street

Leonard Cohen chose the life of a monk, entering the monastic life at the *Mount Baldy Zen Center* in the San Gabriel Mountains of California. Retired from his music career, he found himself penniless, swindled by his manager. He was cheated and betrayed, the ATM did not honor his debit card nor did his credit cards work. Aghast, he had nothing left to his name and nothing to leave behind as inheritance for his family.

Back on Boogie Street marked a highly successful late-career comeback tour, Cohen successfully rebuilt his fortune from the success of this tour. What makes Cohen's comeback inspiring is his enthusiasm and focus on his core strengths as a musician and the courage to revisit the road. While he did win a lawsuit against his manager who stole from him, it was the success of the tour that placed him back on a path to good fortune.

We cannot always prevent ourselves from hurdles that come our way. Entrepreneurial careers are particularly prone to setbacks, bred from a host of reasons such as conflicting interests, infighting, rivalry, bruised egos, competition, the list is endless. It can be impossible to safeguard against everything when running a small start-up. The losses must be viewed against the full spectrum of future possibilities. It pays to remodel and rebuild centering around core strengths, avoiding further hurdles or choices that digress from strengths and compound losses. Throughout my career I have seen senior leaders and entrepreneurs succumb to pressures and begin unraveling and changing course as the pressure alleviates. Practical drivers can define these decisions. If there are obvious show stoppers and red flags, it may be better to avoid such alliances that are headed for a breakdown. Short term steps under pressure usually lead to further losses and worse still, a loss of reputation. It takes some ingenuity and resolve to arrive at a more favorable and sustainable agreement. A clear focus on core, undisputed strengths, seeking support from friends along the path, as advocated by William Green, with solidarity, can make the comeback on anyone's Boogie Street worthwhile.

Culture as Support

The passing of loved ones is the worst loss of all. Losing friendships and relationships that matter comes a close second. Protecting ourselves at moments where the heart cries out becomes an imperative. Diane Ackerman describes darkness that may engulf us as "flying down narrow alleyways on leather wings," with "sticky webs across the sky," protecting ourselves from such darkness can become an emergency.

I am not the first to turn to culture as a crutch when struck by adversity. While a prisoner in Auschwitz, the Italian writer Primo Levi, used poetry to stay anchored. On one occasion, he tried to recall the cantos of Dante's *The Divine Comedy* and share the verse with his fellow inmates. When he forgot a few lines he was frustrated and exclaimed: "I would give today's soup to know how to connect 'the like on any day' to the last lines." The beauty in verse became a means of survival for Primo Levi.

We can be hit by a series of adverse developments. There can be a domino effect and confluence of bad news. You lose your job, your wife leaves you, your children spiral downwards in school, your health suffers, you become bitter and negative, you find it hard to come out of the abyss. In any such vicious cycle we turn to our default survival mechanism—close friends, family, mentors who can put us back on track, our financial reserves, even if they may not be endless, our inner reserves of character. What do you do if you find that your friends were really business associates who left along with your high-paying job, that you do not have much by way of family or community, and that your financial reserves are depleted by the long wait? Building new ties from a place of weakness may be much harder than from a place where you could confidently showcase your strengths. At such times, culture and strength of character can help you find your way out of the darkness. I was fortunate to receive such guidance early in life, I did not grow up with organized faith but had the opportunity to build inner reserves of culture like a tap root that ran deep. As I evolved, the root spread and entwined with design, protecting me from passing storms and guiding me towards solutions.

Raymond Williams, the Welsh writer and a prominent voice in Cultural Studies, describes culture as being ordinary. He urges us to celebrate the quotidian. Williams was raised in a working class family in Wales. He earned his admission into an elite institution through good grades. He never felt overwhelmed by the superiority of Cambridge University despite his humble roots. He could find common meaning between his childhood, traditions and the fine learning he received at Cambridge. We can undermine the influence of culture by placing it as some lofty form of entitlement. Williams warns against such snobbery. He likens it to reaching for a "gun, wallet or argot," symbols of power that intimidate and create distance.

Weaving culture into our everyday life lets us sort and refer to our thoughts in our interactions with others. It gives us a different form of influence, one that connects and consoles with our inner strength. In our interactions with others, culture lends itself to interpretation, to understand differing backgrounds and orientation, sometimes referred to as cultural codes. In anthropology, culture refers to whatever is distinctive about the way of life of a people. In cultural anthropologist James Clifford's treatise, *The Predicament of Culture*, he suggests that it can be helpful to sometimes break the codes:

> I am concerned less with charting intellectual or artistic traditions than with following some of the byways of what I take to be a crucial modern orientation toward cultural order. If I sometimes use familiar terms against the grain, my aim is to cut across retrospectively established definitions.

Clifford adds about experiential knowledge of culture:

> Based on a feel for the foreign context, a kind of accumulated savvy and a sense of style of a people or place. Such an appeal is frequently explicit in the texts of the early professional participant-observers. Margaret Mead's claim to grasp the underlying principle or ethos of a culture through a heightened sensitivity to form, tone, gesture, and behavioral styles, and Malinowski's stress on his life in the village and the comprehension derived from the imponderabilia of daily existence, are prominent cases in point.

At a business level, throughout my consulting and coaching career, I have been queried on the importance of culture fit. Companies can place a high premium on someone who fits their culture. As I evolve my relationship with designing a cultural experience, I view culture as separate from compatibility. Compatibility is vital for any relationship to work well, be it personal or business. Whereas diversity of culture may actually fuel innovation and bring a fresh perspective. We need not be similar culturally yet we can be sensitive to another's cultural orientation, it is important to be compatible but not necessary to commit to the same culture. We can limit ourselves if we take an exclusive view of culture and can expand our cultural influence by embracing diversity. Edwin Markham's words drive the point home:

> He drew a circle that shut me out—
> Heretic, rebel, a thing to flout.
> But love and I had the wit to win:
> We drew a circle and took him in!
> ~ Edwin Markham

I learned about Stouffer Hotels from an investor and colleague in my prior firm, who is part of the Stouffer family. Stouffer Hotels was a luxury hotel chain that was part of Nestlé. The hotels existed under the Stouffer banner from the 1960s till 1996, close to thirty years. Stouffer Hotels was known for its deep culture which served as a glue with employees at all levels of the company. Nestlé sold the business in 1996 and the hotels changed ownership, finally integrating with Marriott Hotels. Despite the passage of two decades since the demise of Stouffer Hotels, the culture continues to live through former employees, who continue to recount stories and celebrate the nostalgia. When culture withstands death and enters the everyday, continuing to serve as a glue for relationships, it offers us much more than a brand or a title. It can travel and live on under a new name and spread its influence.

Displacement, be it professional or personal, can bring losses, and at such intersections our cultural underpinnings can help us through the abyss. Political displacements such as asylum seekers and refugees are known to lose everything, yet they carry their culture, their food, their folklore and their customs, and this becomes a way for them to rebuild their life, despite losses, in a new land.

My relationship with culture when suffering from loss or grief is similar to faith. I find comfort in the arts, literature, poetry, composition—the same way others may find in meditation, spirituality or scripture. I refer to examples from history or fiction, such as characters in a Shakespearean play or a musical composition, not dissimilar to Primo Levi turning to Dante in Auschwitz and Nelson Mandela recounting lines from William Henley's *Invictus*. My design canvas is informed by culture—designing an experience can be all to do with personality, references, feelings, story, and the various ingredients that make up a cultural fabric. I have practiced this with clients and more intimately, in my personal life, with members of my family. The intersection of design and culture can be an influential experience that offers us stability to withstand loss and not only secure us from a disruptive downfall, but expand and enrich our future.

EIGHT

Playtime

I am closer to death today than I was yesterday. With every breath I take, death draws nigh. Not just for me but for everyone. By our sheer existence, we come closer to death with every second that passes.

> I watched him almost sculpted against the pillar
> day after month after year
> Unchanging except for the grey which outgrew
> the black of his hair
> "Good Morning"—the absent touch to his cap,
> the nod
> were the only signs that he was alive against the
> pillar
> Suddenly he was not there anymore
> There was shuffling of a vacant seat somewhere
> in my memory
> I gazed at the pillar sculpted into permanence
> against the emptiness
>
> ~ *Death,* Shakuntala Hawoldar

Approximately 8,460 people die every day in the United States according to the Centers for Disease Control and Prevention. Someone is killed by a gun every ten hours in California per the Department of Justice. It is a miracle that we are alive even as death stares at us in plain sight. There is reason to live our fullest life, with gratitude, for every day that we are alive.

Designing holidays and retreats was what I did for a good part of my twenties. There was a kind of rush in bringing pleasure to people. The experience was what mattered the most—not the destination nor the tourist spots. These were important, but what people enjoyed the most was the total experience. People save, plan and wait for such special moments and expect excellence. One missing piece could destroy the whole experience. I learned early in my professional life that small touches and attentiveness can make a big difference in elevating the experience beyond the life of the holiday or retreat. The steps were enacted with spit, polish and shine every time—building the mood in advance with the help of film or literature, conversations began to flow, unfolding the experience gracefully and creating memories that would be honored in scrapbooks, souvenirs and gifts, cherished for future reference. What would be remembered more effortlessly were the unexpected personalized touches. As part of the preparation, I would sometimes send a book of verse by Rilke, with a scent strip as a bookmark that I may have picked up at a department store, in the perfume section, which I would inscribe with a passing greeting, in a playful periwinkle blue. Such pleasant fussiness was not only acknowledged but celebrated.

The more challenging part was the retention of the experience once back at work. Even the most pleasant memories from a holiday or retreat would seldom travel into the hustle and bustle of everyday life. Unlike Wordsworth, it would be hard to reconnect "with a host of golden daffodils," while on a couch back home "in vacant or in pensive mood." It was wonderful to design magnificent experiences and partake of them without expectations that they would be therapeutic interludes amid our normal routine, once back home. These experiences were seldom glamorous companions for the mundane. Ironically, I would remember pleasant dinner experiences when I would be at another pleasant dinner, or fancy holidays when I would be on holiday, but would never recall a dinner or a holiday while doing my laundry, driving to work, buying groceries or executing other routine chores. Wordsworth was wrong—in his verse, "I Wandered Lonely as a Cloud," he shares that the memory of a "host of golden daffodils" would perk him up when he would be idle or bored, but memories from pleasant holidays would seldom appear in my mind's eye in the midst of routine activities, as much as I love Wordsworth's poetry.

Every Day Counts

It was later in life that I could relate to expressions like those of Mark Twain: "Find a job you enjoy doing, and you will never have to work a day in your life." Making our everyday life count for the days we have left to live, becomes an imperative, for ourselves and all those we serve. We need to offer the best version of ourselves to those we serve. Our spirit must shine through like a smile that travels to the eyes and is felt, not just viewed.

I am fortunate to have mainly lived by such intention and when I found myself on the wrong road I could find the support to pave one that was directed closer to my aspirations. It is true that we sometimes have to make peace by adjusting to something we may not love and find other reasons to be happy. The tension between what we do and what we wish to do may persist. At any point, if we find ourselves trapped in a place where our very existence is compromised, then leaving such a place is better than hanging on. In the course of my professional life, executives have sought my advice on what to prioritize in their careers. I have always erred in favor of the total package—consideration must be given to health and family, not only a high-paying job at the cost of everything else. The spark that lights us must always be kindled through our work or outside our work by an outlet that connects us to our passion, something that we live for.

Play for the Everyday

If we come to the realization that every day matters, we can find ways to situate ourselves in environments where we are in sync with our surroundings. Be it with family, friends, or an employer, who enables us to make our days purposeful and pleasant. We cannot help but acknowledge play as always delivering on its promise of pleasure. Weaving play into the everyday is a sustainable way to find happiness alongside grand moments that may be welcome yet occur infrequently.

Play is easy to recognize yet hard to define. In the article *The Elements of Play: Toward a Philosophy and Definition of Play,* Scott Eberle shares, "at its most elemental, play always promises fun. He goes on to add that humans and animals alike, are programmed for play:

> Because other mammals play, it is exceedingly unlikely that this talent arose spontaneously in our own species as a feature of our exclusive property right. No, play is widely shared and adaptive and, in fact, has enhanced the survival of our graduating class—mammals—over the very long haul.

Play in business settings is increasingly gaining recognition for its role in creating a satisfying work culture that attracts and retains employees. Play can foster innovation, making it instrumental in organizational learning and development. Brendan Boyle, an authority on play and Founder of IDEO's Play Lab, is a proponent of play in daily behaviors of work life: "I help instill a playful culture, not only in mindset, but also in daily behaviors. Play allows us to experiment, empathize and take creative risks. It keeps us engaged in our projects and makes us better innovators." Perhaps the most viable way for us to incorporate play into our daily lives is by encouraging a creative culture. Small gestures that exercise this muscle, from the way we tie our shoelaces to the way we greet someone or send a message, need never be outlandish or rude yet can be playful and send our neurons buzzing. Although not fully aware of the science behind it, I do feel buzzed and energetic when I see others engage in such activities.

Play as a Foundation for Learning

Emory Lee's research at the University of Melbourne, Victoria, titled, *Believing in Artistic Making and Thinking, Studies in Art Education,* uncovers the foundational role of belief and the interconnectedness between play, thinking, and making among children. A group of ten children, between the age group of 10-12 (with an equal number of boys and girls) were selected from a class of thirty-five to be observed in tasks of art, craft, dance, drama, music, and writing. Key findings include that the children wished for affirmation along three areas: social interaction, transformation, and representation. A fourth area, belief, emerged as pivotal to the thinking and making process. Belief propelled the child in picking one direction over the other, recognizing the presence of a problem, and seeking a solution to remedy the problem. Belief can be interpreted as confidence to experiment on an intuitive desire or impulse. Play drove the manipulation of form and image towards finding solutions. Belief served as a catalyst in the choices exercised by the children and became central to peer-teacher recognition through social interaction and representation. The choice and application of art, transformative by its very nature, was also tied to belief or the confidence to experiment with an idea.

Researchers from La Trobe University in Melbourne observed the Thinking and Making exercises of the children over a twelve-month period. The classes were held in dynamic settings where unpredictable outcomes were desired and encouraged. Social interaction, representation, and transformation were at the center of the thinking and making process in all art forms. External validation was an important determinant for the students. They were motivated by: How may I make something that my peers and teachers will accept? Transformation served as a label signifying that all artistic making involved the changing of form. Representation stood for portrayal of some phenomena or experience. The students were encouraged to digress from patterning and embrace ideas and feelings instead. The ability of the child to shift from literal to abstract or metaphoric, involved three areas: preferences of the child, unexpressed viewpoint, and individual approach or style. Belief was described as vital to the exercise:

> Belief becomes a shared experience.
> The product then cannot be
> the result of mere self-indulgent action, but
> becomes an appropriate
> and meaningful process within a given context.
> Belief is thus personal
> and shared. It is for this reason that the child
> shows her work to her
> parents or teacher for approval; for approval
> is a stamp.

The observation opens the door to the notion that belief includes more than the individual and that play can be part of collective craftsmanship or workmanship. Such an approach was encouraged as flexibility opened the door to options and the willingness to consider new ideas. Play became a medium for working towards goals. Play emerged as a dynamic term where: "individuals have the capacity to manipulate phenomena and change realities." The influence of role play exists not only in the realm of childhood, but also in adult life, as part of her research

Emery Lee discovered that:

> Sporting contests, public ceremonies and politics may be serious adult activities. Yet all involve pretending to abide by the rules and playing roles. Game playing, selection and role performance may be both fact and fiction in adult life, as they are in childhood. Thus Erikson suggests that people are never more human than when they play.

Further observations by Scott Eberle include:

> Much of the pleasure we derive from play is social in nature, and play strengthens our social skills. Play propagates itself in our close groups, strengthening old acquaintanceships and rewarding us with new friendships. These bonds shore up our societies with common associations, common experiences, and common purposes. Playing also deliberately rearranges our relationships and so enhances our social wit. At play we learn to read others' intentions. And by playing we learn to deflect and defuse conflict. This is how play contributes to our composure and ease, and this composure, in turn, spreads to our social circles.

I decided to study play in more detail as an experience that could be designed for the everyday.

New York in December

It had snowed the night before. Early December in New York is cold and warm. The dressy streets and festive windows offer a warm welcome diffusing the winter chill. The snow-clad streets never fail to invite a brisk walk, the color from storefronts mingled with freshly fallen snow create a live Christmas Card, to be experienced with every step down the street. I made my way through the snow from Lafayette Street to Fulton Street. I was meeting a colleague at Cafe Greene Grape in Brooklyn. I arrived about half an hour early that crisp, cold morning and ordered a steamy latte. The languid strains of Leonard Cohen's "Famous Blue Raincoat" melted into the air like silky marmalade on toast, bittersweet and melancholy in the cozy cafe. "Ah, the last time we saw you you looked so much older your famous blue raincoat was torn at the shoulder, you'd been to the station to meet every train and you came home without Lili Marlene."

"Hello," my colleague interrupted my thoughts. "Shall we move to the table by the window?"

We were meeting to discuss LEGO Serious Play. My colleague, who was part of Design Research at NYU's Tisch School of the Arts, was in the midst of being commissioned by the Mayor's office to draw up a plan for play, through LEGO, for everyday New Yorkers. The L train was to be grounded for repairs and it was anticipated that this would cause stress and disruption to the daily commute on the busy Brooklyn-Manhattan line. I was impressed by such enlightened leadership that was willing to sponsor creativity and play in the public realm to circumvent urban stress. LEGO Serious Play workshops could provide a forum to contain and process the anger and frustration through creativity and playful design.

LEGO Serious Play provides a reference for a play system built to unlock the imagination of a child, which has been successfully adopted into business and corporate forums. The 3D models built by participants at a workshop, become the footing for group brainstorms, including problem solving and storytelling. Davis Levine, a service designer from Canada, shares that LEGO Serious Play allows the hands to do the thinking, thereby allowing truth over verbal manipulation. People are often afraid of drawing as they worry what others may think of their artistic skills. Through this 3D medium, the fear of the design looking bad is eliminated and the thought behind the creation can become central. Lee shares, "Everyone builds a model and everyone tells a story."

Energy Despite Fatigue

I have experienced play as a way to alleviate stress on more than one occasion. In the context of my inquiry, I had taken a course at Parson's School of Design during the fall of 2018, titled *Critical Fashion Social Justice* and had worked on an assignment called *Drawn to Fear*. My cohort were young and dynamic, mainly in their twenties and early thirties. Designed as a children's coloring book, the assignment investigated serious social and political issues. A series of workshops tied to arguments on social justice, exclusion, bullying, and violence—specifically the ubiquitous influence of fast fashion on aesthetic violence— were expressed through images and games. While they illustrated the severity of the concepts, they were tempered by lighthearted humor, conveying something similar to political caricatures. Heavy discussions found a playful voice through craft and drawings. The cohort met late evenings every Thursday. Despite the hour and fatigue, the element of play created interest and energy. Play was instrumental in lifting the mood and easing fatigue, even when the subject and conversations were difficult.

Play formed an important part of my thesis that eventually led to the Design Studio workshop. The workshop involved thinking, making and communicating the idea within a small, curated cohort.

March 2020: Our World Stood Changed

The pandemic swooped down on us like a black swan. You could hear a pin drop in New York. Not a soul at Grand Central Station—beautiful, empty, with phantoms who could be angels or ghosts, depending on Governor Cuomo's daily address. Some days, the death toll mounted and on other days it waned. The Design Studio workshop, conceived at the Parsons School of Design, New York, was meant to be a sensory, brick and mortar experience but made its debut as a digital interface in the early, uncertain days of the pandemic, when the world went into a silent shack, isolated and sheltered in place. The Design Studio was a hit with the business executive community. The thinking and making studio elements in small cohorts were designed for play and ideation. Everyone loved the small curated sessions with an eclectic participant profile. The creative energy was palpable even without all the sensory elements of a physical encounter. The feedback was consistent—workshops in a studio format were "energizing and far more engaging than a typical networking event," shared a CEO from a B2B company that supports the apparel industry.

What became evident was our innate desire for craft, play and conversations. People actually like to draw and craft once the stage is set and they feel safe within the group. As with a dinner table conversation, much rests on the host, to put guests at ease and enable a smooth flow. Likewise, we could see the "creative confidence," espoused by the original founders of IDEO, come into play, in what came to be known as the *Executive Design Studio,* a series of workshops for professionals, styled as studios. Play served as a social lubricant and a precursor for expression.

In *The Wizard of Oz,* Dorothy, the Scarecrow, the Tin Man and the Cowardly Lion all had different wishes. To allow a diverse set of ideas, the participants at the Design Studio had the freedom to choose their medium of expression, to express their distinct wish. While most preferred to write, draw, or share a visual, there was nothing to stop them from performing a short skit or a song, within their allocated time.

Play is different from structured sport because it can be improvised and creative. You can form your own expression within a broader framework. There is less restriction on the medium you choose and no anxiety of letting a team down. Play can be designed for ideation and conversations—it can be applicable to a range of contexts, and thus, be accessible to everyone.

An integration of play in the everyday can make our days far more pleasant and less reliant on grand memories to escape from boredom. Happiness need not be an occasional interlude if we can lean into play more frequently.

NINE

R e b o o t

Reboot is a term commonly used to reload the operating system of a computer. It also means a refresh or a restart. When it comes to human life, a reboot usually follows an uncomfortable life event, whether it's a breakdown or some other form of displacement or rupture. Sometimes this can be self-induced, and at other times, it is caused by factors outside of our control. And yet, despite the help a reboot can offer, I have never understood the idea of closure. The mind rarely forgets. Memories occupy different chambers of our psyche, the pleasant and the painful. Our instincts are wired for survival and we file the more painful memories away, yet they can pop up to haunt us unexpectedly, like shadows on the wall, when awake and lonely at 2am, or in a dream we rouse from and are unable to shake.

A reboot without memories would be an empty vessel, numb to the past and incapable of embracing a promising future. Ghosts of the living and the dead travel with us in memory. I resonate with Elie Wiesel's sentiment: "To forget the dead would be akin to killing them a second time."I would like to extend this thought to include the living, who may sometimes belong in an altered present. Anyone with a romantic predisposition can relate to nostalgia. Don Draper captured it well in *Mad Men:* "In Greek, 'nostalgia' literally means 'the pain from an old wound.' It's a twinge in your heart far more powerful than memory alone. This device isn't a spaceship, it's a time machine. It goes backwards and forwards, it takes us to a place where we ache to go again." History, with its rich archives and chronicles, can offer us reference points that can help guide a life reboot into an unknown future.

On the threshold of womanhood somewhere between sixteen, going on seventeen, I had read the novel *Bright Day* by J.B. Priestly. Although much of my life was yet to unfold, the nostalgic storyline, entwined with the protagonist's new life, touched me in interesting ways. In later life, I could relate more deeply, from personal experience, to what had once fed my juvenilia. *Bright Day* is set in two periods, post-WWII and pre-WWI. With about two decades separating the two protracted upheavals, the protagonist's early youth is full of merriment in the golden age of England pre-WWI, while the post-WWII period of the story is marked by change and industry. Our protagonist finds himself reconstructing his new life, yet blighted with nostalgia. The periods of his pre-war youth and the disruption from war serve as bookends, reservoirs to draw upon as he constructs his future.

In the book, the protagonist, Gregory Dawson, finds himself in the present, as a stale, disillusioned scriptwriter in Hollywood. To avoid distractions while writing a script, he holes himself up in a nondescript hotel where he is haunted by a rush of deja vu when two encounters send him back on a memory trail to the Bradford of his youth—a chance meeting with a stranger and a performance by a trio of musicians at the hotel. Dawson, the protagonist, who is in fact Priestly's surrogate, recalls:

> It was the slow movement of Schubert's B flat major trio, as I knew at once when the cello began its exquisite quiet tone, slowly and gravely rocking in its immeasurable tenderness. A few moments later, when the cello went wandering to murmur its regret and the violin with its piercing sweetness curved and rocked the same little tune, I was far away, deep in a lost world and a lost time.

Priestly had to escape the ghosts of the past to build his literary career, yet it is the ghosts who made *Bright Day* and his future possible, not in the flesh but in learning, recollection and reimagining. Nostalgia for him was not a return to Bradford but the capacity to feel, to reconnect and to be sensitive. Priestly straddles the ghosts of the past without a loss of optimism for the future. As he shares, "I have always been delighted at the prospect of a new day, a fresh try, one more start, with perhaps a bit of magic waiting somewhere behind the morning." In our rush to gain some mystical closure, we may underestimate the value of nostalgia while keeping up the optimism for a new day.

In some ways, my life as a successful corporate executive can denote a golden pre-war period, followed by an entrepreneurial, vibrant, post-war chapter, from which I find myself rebooting, Priestly-like, towards a future where I take steps back and forth, with ghosts stirred by new encounters and relationships that may still belong in a new rainbow. The wisdom of Peter Pan offers us the important insight: "God gave us memory so that we might have roses in December." Moving forward while cherishing our memories can bring us warmth in an unknown future.

Room for Rescue

Business closures can come with all the roughness of post-war destruction without much of the infusion of resources needed to reconstruct. We may need to take steps back to reconnect and resource a meaningful future. Survival and utilitarian priorities can dominate our present and any form of dalliance or self-indulgence can be viewed as capricious. Being wasteful or irresponsible is never recommended yet survival must involve more than the physical. Rescuing our soul may be as vital to progress, to preserve the spark that makes us worthwhile. Such no man's land for soul rescue in the wasteland of post-business closure becomes a refuge and a luxury. Think of the ice mansion near the fictional town of Yuriatin in the Ural Mountains where Doctor Zhivago began writing his *Lara* poems in the midst of the Russian Revolution. The soul of the entrepreneur carries the passion that makes a business successful—dampening of the soul may lead one to become the living dead.

The biggest challenge in a reboot from entrepreneurship can be finding the luxury to reconnect and rekindle the soul, and the resources needed to do this. Mother Theresa had famously said that she was concerned, not about food and blankets for orphaned children, but for toys and stories that are important to a child's imagination. Too many benefactors get busy feeding and clothing the child without worrying about his imagination. The same can hold true for entrepreneurial rescue, the necessities beyond food and shelter may be elusive and viewed as unnecessary luxuries, and partaking of such luxuries are ridden with guilt, even when they may hold the key to a promising future. Maslow's need hierarchy comes into full force, but sometimes one only addresses survival without aspirations to move beyond that state and to live more fully. You may find a way to survive that may not be a good fit, you get exhausted, your dreams are dead, and the pyramid does not mobilize upwards. You have already lost time and money and all you have at hand is survival and a future with further losses. Not everyone may relate to this but I strongly believe that one should bypass such a doom loop. The spark, energy and capability that led you to entrepreneurship are billable and valuable qualities. Situating where they are appreciated and allowing yourself to reboot unapologetically without distractions is worth pursuing with singular focus.

Within my limited means I have always tried to create room for upliftment, to sharpen my skills and prevent my soul from death and myself from unworthiness. A cocktail of resourcefulness and investments have opened hidden opportunities. People, sponsorships and precious objects have made it possible for me to write these essays, for example, in the midst of a reboot. A client's kindness, a considerate landlord, a loan against a small piece of jewelry I bought in good times, all formed part of the rescue.

The give and take of kindness is the most valuable asset in a reboot. The kinder we can be to ourselves and others, the more value we can bring to our work. It takes many shoulders to get to our destination, we need to be honorable about acknowledging such support from our investors, clients and colleagues. Paying it forward, and equally, paying it back, becomes an obligation. We may not be able to keep to our promises as promptly as we may wish to in a reboot, but maintaining a log is a good practice in order to hold ourselves accountable, to progress responsibly, and to do unto others as we would like done unto us. Situating ourselves appropriately to meet these obligations, despite the odds, is vital for a reboot.

In the Shadow of Rip Van Winkle

The folklore of *Rip Van Winkle,* can be true in many entrepreneurial reboots. After my last firm shut down, whilst I was preoccupied with building a new business model, it was industry and not Rip's fabled slumber that kept me insulated from the world around me. When I emerged with new learnings, the world predating my entrepreneurial life stood changed. Finding a way back had hurdles, as did a way forward. Some call such an intersection a fork in the road. I found it more like a maze from which an opening had to be found for a new entry, or even a reentry. Going back to school was the refuge from where a road could emerge.

Sometimes reboots can entail a few twists and turns, lengthy periods of waiting. The saying, even a good surfer without a wave can easily become inept, holds truth. I found myself insulated, stranded and clutching onto ribbons of optimism,—there was no room for complacency but plenty for caution. "It is the bright day that brings forth the adder," is an important line from *Julius Caesar*. We need to keep up our spirits but not all days that appear to be bright, are truly so. The library of Shakespearean tragedies and comedies have an ongoing relevance, particularly in entrepreneurial reboots. When surrounded by doom and gloom, we have to assiduously work to steer towards happy endings, even when we are unsure if the road we are on leads that way.

Business and Relationship Breakdowns

The same can hold true for relationship breakdowns. Business closures and relationship failures have a hand-in-glove connection. Too often, a failure at work results in a void where old friends may leave and new ones may be hard to find. Breakdowns in personal, intimate relationships that may have mattered can be particularly painful. In the novel *Chéri* by Colette and in the 2009 film adaptation of the book, there is a catchy sentiment expressed by the lead character Léa on returning to Paris after a long period of absence. Her old life and identity are gone and she finds herself out of step with the changes:

> Being with someone in a long relationship is like
> following your husband to the colonies.
> By the time you got back you've forgotten
> what you're supposed to wear,
> and nobody remembers who you are
> ~ Colette, from Chéri

When I returned to Los Angeles, where I had run my firm after a period of absence, it just wasn't the Paris of my heyday anymore. The places were still the same but my relationships had changed. I was living in transitional new digs. Returning to familiar spots and neighborhoods brought a flood of memories but the inhabitants were new. I grasped for straws, for my old tailor or hairdresser, a warm greeting here or there. I was confronted by a harsh new reality within the familiarity of the old.

In my many years listening to professionals who may be coming out of a long-standing relationship or a professional breakdown, I have found such sentiment echoed. The partner or spouse who is left to navigate a new reality may feel a similar obstacle as Colette's Léa in *Chéri*, returning to a changed Paris.

Nostalgia is not wasted sentimentalism, nor is it a sign of weakness and a yearning to refabricate failure—it is a way to be attuned with our feelings, to be grounded in the deepest safeties of our heart. The day we become uncaring and unfeeling, we lose our human touch and the power to connect with others, an important quality for finding our way back to where we belong. Without feelings, our soul dies, and without a soul we may as well be dead.

Reboots in Midlife

Singapore does not have much of a coastline—there are a few places that offer seafood specialties close to the water. It was a typically wet and humid evening in June of 2004. My former colleague and mentor had arranged a small dinner gathering at the East Coast Lagoon Village. The invite said, "Join us for pepper crabs and Tiger beer." The village is a basic hawker center selling spicy street food, where locals, tourists and expatriates can be found eating noodles and seafood with a range of juices, teas and the very popular Tiger beer drunk from large, frosty beer mugs. I was seated next to a distinguished older gentleman, who was Tom, my host's guest of honor and the reason behind the impromptu dinner.

I entered the conversation on midlife career paths without trepidation. As an advisor to executives, I felt this was my forte. Midway through the meal, my colleague drew me aside and whispered in my ear.

"You are doing great adding your insights, you do know you are sitting next to Elliott, right?"

"Elliott who?" I innocently responded.

"Elliott Jacques is the man who coined the phrase 'mid-life crisis.' Before his research, it was an unknown term."

I was awestruck and did most of the listening for the rest of the evening. I later learned from my colleague that Elliott was impressed by me and had left me an inscribed copy of his book, *Death and the Midlife Crisis*.

The theory on midlife crises has evolved over the years with improved quality of life, a host of new opportunities powered by technology and other emerging fields, including improved healthcare and longevity. Today, there is increased public discourse on mental wellbeing and the acceptance of work/life balance in many industries, this has changed how we perceive the concept of a midlife crisis. We don't live in such collective denial about the implications of professional stress. My opinion on this subject is that midlife crisis can strike at any point and usually accompanies a fear of wasted time with a desire to accomplish some goal before it is too late. It is marked by anxiety and disquiet that can descend at any age. For a sports star or a model, midlife could be in their late twenties, for someone in the creative field, maturation of concepts may occur later in life. Henri Matisse's best work happened later in his career.

I had the pleasure of meeting Chip Conley recently. He has authored the book, *The Midlife Chrysalis,* I relate to his view of midlife being a period of awakening, where our leanings can transform us towards a beautiful place of awareness and opportunity. This is particularly true of creative and intellectual pursuits, I have seldom enjoyed the works of an artist, musician, author or entrepreneur in their salad days, the work improves significantly with maturity. We can appreciate their expression better and the linkages that led to their progression.

Despite greater acceptance of an extended midlife, the relevance of quality and time grows in importance. We hit a timeline where wasting a window or entering the wrong door can easily escalate into a waste of a lifetime.

Reboots in midlife need thoughtful positioning. There is no easy answer, we can only control what is within our influence. Self-awareness is a good place to start—what is it that we are good at and enjoy doing? The next question could be situational—where could we honestly say that we are purposeful and not wasting a day in our life? A reboot is a precious opportunity. We owe ourselves answers to these two questions with brutal honesty. A healthy compromise is always an option if what we lose is compensated by something that we gain in tangible value. Are we fulfilling some other personal goal that is important, possibly related to family? Is the role well-compensated, so we can fast track other obligations? Is the location someplace special with other fringe benefits? There could be a sound list of reasons for a healthy compromise that still keeps us on the path towards where we need to go.

Repositioning for Marketability

The biggest question can be positioning ourselves as marketable and worthy of investment despite the setback of closure or failure. All else being equal, the biggest learning from a setback is your ability to cope with adversity. In his book, *Richer, Wiser, Happier,* William Green points to the correlation between success and our ability to cope with adversity. Leaders who have demonstrated such mental toughness command a premium beyond those who may have thrived in peaceful and comfortable conditions. Our ability to communicate our setbacks as a learning and our capability for overcoming adversity becomes an asset.

Design theorists Horst Rittel and Melvin Webber coined the expression "wicked problem" to describe complex, unstructured problems with no apparent right or wrong answer. Such problems are unique by their very nature. A midlife professional reboot can quickly become a wicked problem unless we approach it with self-awareness. Our wish list paired with our threshold for compromise, along with learning from adversity, becomes a feather in our cap. We can demonstrate our ability to cope and rise above adversity from a business setback, and we consequently become valuable in situations that need such skills. Having a clear direction and communicating this message clearly is foundational to designing a midlife reboot. The same framework can be applied with minor adjustments to personal relationships, too.

Getting Centered

Sometimes designing a reboot experience can defy reason. "Life can be a tale told by an idiot, full of sound and fury, signifying nothing," said Macbeth. We will never know when senseless tragedy may strike us. Thus, my emphasis is on rescuing the soul and honoring the significance of each day of our life. If we can be diligent with what matters most: our family, our health, a few things that make us happy so we may spread happiness, we can count ourselves as fortunate. Preserving such a status quo while working to improve all the rest is reason enough to celebrate the gift of life:

> And whatever your labors and aspirations,
> in the noisy confusion of life,
> keep peace in your soul.
> With all its sham, drudgery and broken dreams,
> It is still a beautiful world.
> Be cheerful. Strive to be happy
> $\sim$ The Desiderata

No design for a reboot experience can be perfect. All we can do is center ourselves with the foundational values of what we like doing, and can excel at. We should not shy away from monetizing such skills optimally while not compromising on what matters most to us. Above all else, we must ensure that our soul is nourished in our striving for happiness—for ourselves, and for those we serve.

TEN

Ambience

The early 2000s were marked by exotic travel for our family. I had planned a trek to Borneo via the east Malaysian corridor of Sarawak with my son, to spend one week in the deep interiors of the rainforest. It was a life-changing experience. There were no tourists, only the occasional environmentalist or photographer at the trailhead. Just us and a local indigenous guide from the Dayak tribe. Our days would start early and end just before sunset. We were in the lap of nature, the air was pure, the forest resplendent with every shade of green, and we would hold onto living serpentine roots while climbing. This was the home of the Orangutan and the Proboscis Monkey. The Rafflesia flower was in full bloom, carnivorous plants feasted on insects, unpolluted beaches were strewn with drift wood and small marine creatures, and the trees felt like they touched the sky. This was paradise—and for us, it was experiencing the embrace of Mother Nature. On the third day of our trek, our guide asked us in broken English.

"Where you live?"

"Singapore," I said.

"Who take care of your house?"

"No one, we locked it, Singapore is safe," I said.

"So when you return and open the door, how will the energy say hello to you?"

I thought of all the times I have returned to open a place that had been locked for a period of time and the unwelcoming energy that had greeted me when I opened the door. It was always an unwelcome hello.

"Not nice hello," I said. Our Dayak guide went on, "we come to the forest every morning, how does the forest greet you?"

"Beautiful and welcoming every morning," my son chimed in and nodded in agreement. Our guide went on profoundly: "trees that are a hundred years old greet you, fresh, welcoming like a new day. A new apartment locked up for one week greets you like it is stale and dead."

I have held this simple yet sage observation from our Dayak guide as a special realization. Being close to nature always gives us a fresh new day, evergreen and pure.

As sentients, our perception of ambience is multisensory. All our senses, sight, sound, smell, touch and taste inform our experience of ambience. We process our experience with the world through our senses. Experiencing the rainforest and the intense intimacy of nature presents ambience at its very best, our primal sensory selves in the lap of Mother Nature.

In his essay Urban Futures In The Age of Unsettlement, Tony Fry calls attention to nature:

> The future is not empty; it is not a void. Rather it is filled with all those things we have thrown into it as they travel back toward us delivering either their futuring or defuturing potential. In this respect, we travel toward the future while the future travels toward us.

Fry adds:

> While recognition of environmental problems has increased over the last fifty years, and while climate change has become a fear of the age, our demands upon, and abuse of, those environments that sustain us continue almost unabated. In the face of that deep unknowing embedded in

anthropocentrism. ——We cannot cease to be anthropocentric. But the more we recognise this and take responsibility for what we do, the more time we will have (and the less damage we will do).

The trek to Borneo was a revelation of how pure the ambience could be when we are extremely close to nature. There is a growing consciousness about climate change and sustainable practices in urban circles, yet it is hard to weave nature in all its bounty while designing ambience in urban settings. Yet we can seek small measures, rooftop gardens, ocean fronts, manicured library lawns, botanic gardens and beautifully crafted al fresco dining, with plants under the stars—an oasis in the midst of a concrete jungle.

Al Fresco Dining

"Mr. Puck does not respond to emails," said an uptight voice."If you have a brochure or something in print, please send it over, he will look at it."

Upon this request, I sent across a coffee table book that I had produced with a fine art photographer, a statement piece, above and beyond a standard corporate brochure. Wolfgang Puck's secretary acknowledged my book most graciously, and I knew I had struck a friendly chord with the offices of the celebrity chef and restaurateur.

A couple of months later I had the honor of hosting a prominent Australian executive who was also a public figure on his visit to Los Angeles. I contacted Wolfgang Puck's assistant. His much-celebrated restaurant, Spargo on Beverley Hills was my first choice. Spargo has the most wonderful ambience with food and service to match. Being very popular it can be hard to get the best table at short notice. I did not hesitate to put in a request for a special table in the courtyard, under the stars surrounded by plants. I routed the call through the corporate office instead of the restaurant directly fearing I may be placed on a waitlist.

Los Angeles can be nippy in the evenings and patio heaters are quite popular in open air spaces. We were ushered to an excellent table at Spargo, in the courtyard by the potted bougainvilleas creeping up the cream-colored walls, a ballet of flames dancing beautifully in the fireplace a short distance away—it all made a pretty spectacle. Mr. Puck was doing the rounds at the restaurant that evening, and soon enough he stopped by our table and greeted us warmly. He remembered my book. The ambience tied it all perfectly with a bow. Our VIP guest was pleased and we continued to share a wonderful rapport, several years on.

Ambience is possibly the most important aspect of designing an experience with conversation as a close second. I give ambience the top spot as we can feel ambience and connect with it even before any words are spoken. It sets the mood and tone for the rest of proceedings, be it an event, a casual meeting or an everyday activity.

Ambience for the Everyday

In all my years, advising and coaching senior leaders, I have placed a high emphasis on ambience as a touchstone for building relationships. This includes selecting the right ambience for interviews and onboarding of new leaders. I have been challenged on this order of priority by ultra-practical executives. The hurdles I usually encounter are questions like, why not keep things real and authentic? Shouldn't the people joining us or doing business with us see things in the light of reality? Why dress things up when that would not happen everyday? My modest response has been that relationships are worthy of such investment, the opportunity to do something special does not present itself everyday, why not take advantage of the window and sow seeds for a relationship with a pleasant start. A cold approach could be mechanical and less impactful in developing a relationship within a shorter timespan. A good ambience can put people at ease and allow them to open up and share about themselves in ways they would otherwise not.

Experiences that stir and inspire us to bring forth our best selves lay the foundation for a deeper connection. I have heard it said that people can withstand the mundane and tough times better if they have partaken of good times and benefitted from the warmth they may have received. The positive experience expands their capacity to give even within limited means. They understand the tacit value of engaging fully, harnessing a holistic mindset. Naysayers who may be predisposed to dry routines can spot the difference between good and bad ambience only when they experience good ambience.

As with everything in life, balancing the special with the practical is important, and good design facilitates such orchestration. A design mindset helps us to pick up on ambience as an important detail. Ambience is not only about the extraordinary—small touches like moving a table closer to the window or placing a potted plant by a desk can sometimes make a big difference. Glenn Gissler, a famous New York interior designer, likes to say that when he picks a restaurant, he looks for a beautiful atmosphere, great food but also for a space where "you can hear yourself talk." Every small detail can help improve the ambience.

The designer Victor Papanek's view of design is broad ranging. In his book *Design for the Real World, Human Ecology and Social Change,* he shares that design could be "composing an epic poem, executing a mural, painting a masterpiece, writing a concerto." It could also apply to "educating a child," "baking a pie," or "reorganizing a desk." Such a holistic view of design can intersect with ambience to make everyday experiences meaningful.

Synesthesia

Ambience is mainly a sensory experience. We can discover an unexpected breakthrough from a synesthetic approach. Synesthesia is a neurological condition where one sense can trigger another sense. Synesthetes can taste sounds, hear in color, think in shapes and so on. Sevi Merter of Yaşar University shares in the essay, "Synesthetic Approach in the Design Process for Enhanced Creativity and Multisensory Experiences", that synesthetes and non-synesthetes can both relate to creative disruption. The stimulation passes through the avenue of our senses. Creative people have a higher tolerance for inconsistency, contradiction and paradox than more literal-minded people. Expressions like "cool jazz, sharp cheese, sour note, feeling blue," are just a few synesthetic expressions cited by her. There is no logical connection between the words, yet we sense a connection and understand them perfectly. Merter adds that such expressions add to the sensory experience and are "obvious to both synesthetes and non-synesthetes."

The extreme out of the box nature of synesthesia lends itself to creative exploration. We do not have to be synesthetes to experience senses at a visceral level and flex our creative muscles. A disruptive ambience can inject conditions for creative thinking and ideation which may be less accessible in regular, everyday environments.

Events and workshops held in quirky, unusual locations allow us to think and react differently. A warehouse or a barn, an old train station by the railroad, a medieval castle, are just some alternative examples where the ambience can create disruption for creative thinking. The ambience of a disruptive setting brings a fresh perspective which in turn can cause us to digress from the normative and tune into new unexpected pathways.

The lines from *A Midsummer Night's Dream* by Shakespeare capture the expressiveness of synesthetic thinking:

I have had a most rare vision. I had a dream, past the wit of man to say what dream it was...

The eye of man hath not heard, the ear of man hath not seen, man's hand is not able to taste, his tongue to conceive, nor his heart to report, what my dream was.

In her book *A Natural History of the Senses,* Diane Ackerman shares that our senses allow us to "luxuriate in the spectacle of life." She describes artists as being extrasensory, "Great artists feel at home in the luminous spill of sensation, to which they add their own complex sensory Niagara." She shares a jestful example to do with Picasso: "Picasso's walks in the forests of Fontainebleau, where he got an overwhelming indigestion of greenness which he felt driven to empty onto canvas." Ackerman goes on to add:

Most people think of the mind as being located in the head but the latest findings in physiology suggest that the mind doesn't really dwell in the brain but travels the whole body on caravans of hormone and enzyme, busily making sense of the compound wonders we catalogue as touch, taste, smell, hearing, vision.

The close relationship between our senses and ambience creates openings to sometimes force disruption so we may gain a fresh perspective. Our routine environment may not offer us the same breakthroughs that a new ambience may bring us.

Space and Ambience

The ancient world designed spaces with significance well beyond their basic use. The astronomical alignment found in the pyramids to precisely face north, south, east, and west, the "chi" or life force behind feng shui may vary in modern day scientific interpretation yet offer a unique ambience within the design of the constructed environment.

The Italian Renaissance is known for giving ambience special meaning through structure, ornament and even color, in a quest to connect the physical with the celestial. Architecture was believed to heal, sharpen memory, build civic life, facilitate communication and much more. In his book *Architecture and Memory*, Robert Kirkbride explains the relevance of color in the Renaissance:

> Green, he writes, represents Venus and the Moon, whose moist natures are appropriate to things of birth, such as thoughts. The Apollonian sun is represented by gold, and the jovial influence of Juniper—-vital, Ficino emphasizes to counteract Saturn's melancholy—-is captured by sapphire the color of lapis lazuli and ultramarine. Also effective against Saturn's black bile are coral (red) and chalcedony (milky gray). Elsewhere in the *Book of Life*, Ficino associates purple with a safer, diluted form of Saturn's humor.

Hotels, particularly expensive, luxury properties are known to give ambience a special place when designing an experience. They go to great descriptive lengths to weave the story into architecture, location, comfort, food and beverage and integrate the company's values with the service. Marriott Hotels did away with small shampoo bottles to reduce plastic waste, and consciousness towards sustainability is echoed in the service at their hotels.

Intrigue and artistry hold our fancy, be it the special hue of yellow sofas at the Carlyle, New York or the iconic pink of the Beverley Hills Hotel, every detail is captured and retold to engulf us within their special ambience.

Hospitality in Healthcare

There is an increased interest in the healthcare industry where constructed environments such as hospitals are trying to emulate the hotel experience. Melanie West of the *Wall Street Journal* shares in an article titled "Hotel-Style Hospitality Comes to Hospitals" about hiring former hotel executives from companies like Starwood and the Four Seasons, among other big brands, to overhaul the clinical feel of hospital service and bring personalization and warmth, including the decor, placing real art on walls, playing elevator-style music in corridors, along with other touches of hospitality that mark the crossing over of the hotel experience into hospitals.

The sick bay of my elementary school, located in an obscure hill station of the Himalayas, run by Irish nuns, was very quaint. I still remember the perfectly polished floors, warm yellow lighting from wall sconces, animal lithographs, polished brass fittings and windows overlooking a rose garden. Closer in ambience to a Brownstone in Westchester County than a hospital emergency room. There could be many alluring ways to weave design and ambience in meaningful ways to enhance experiences in hospitals or other anxiety prone settings like a dentist parlour. Much can be done to enhance such environments by raising our consciousness towards ambience.

The Ambience of Pseudoscience

Have you ever felt a gaze on your back and turned around to catch someone looking at you from behind. Almost everyone experienced extrasensory perception or ESP at some point. Likewise have you thought of someone after a long gap, only to find a message from them in your inbox the next day, your thoughts passed in the ether. While it could be mere coincidence, it does spook you and make you wonder about the science of telepathy. A vibe can spell a mood even before any words are spoken. Our ability to perceive and interpret subtle, non-verbal cues like body language, facial microexpressions, vocal tone, and even subtle chemical signals like sweat or hormones, involve subconscious processing by the brain. Our ability to process emotions and memories contribute to how we understand and feel a vibe. Animals are particularly good at picking up on signals and vibes, they can smell danger, sense a storm, and call out an alarm well before we can as humans. Attuning with our animal or primal selves brings us closer to such unexplained scientific phenomena labeled as pseudoscience.

Energy and ambience can be closely connected when intangible experiences like emotional energy contribute towards ambience. Ambience is derived from the Latin word "to go around," meaning the surrounding atmosphere, mood, or sensory environment of a space, which can include both physical qualities and the emotional energy of people within it. Energy in an emotional or intangible form can be interchangeable with ambience and become experiential—this excludes the reference to quantifiable energy such as heat or electricity. We can sense and connect with the energy of a person or space the same way that we do with the atmosphere created by ambience.

Folklore and pseudoscience muddled with design can sometimes give us extraordinary outcomes. My son went back to university some years ago. He had previously dropped out after a year in college to pursue a degree at a renowned music institute in Los Angeles. After a few years of trying to be a musician, he found himself going nowhere and decided to return and finish his undergraduate studies. He had lost touch with reading and writing, and was depressed from what he thought to be a failure as a musician. His grades were below average, he would go to class, unshaven and looking scruffy. But he somehow made it to the final year without dropping out.

I approached him one day and said I needed his help with a design project I was working on. This involved me doing an intermittent photoshoot for about a year and since he was studying business, he would need to look sharp, shaven and well groomed. Some days would involve dressing in business casual and other days, more colorful, casual attire. I dug out examples from Woody Allen movies and other preppy magazines. Family traditions and folklore suggest that demeanor and grooming can send a special positive vibe. Fortunately my son agreed to participate in the project that we titled *rainbow*. The results were remarkable. A well-groomed person with a smile behind a picture taken every other day, led to major improvement in grades and emotional energy, which led to a positive connection with others and the environment.

Chromotherapy or color therapy, is a pseudoscientific practice that uses colors to promote physical, mental, and emotional wellbeing. Color travels in wavelengths that influence our body and brain differently. The effect of project *rainbow* is hard to back with science, other than some gray space of pseudoscience and folklore where emotion and ambience concocted an outcome beyond my expectations. A simple explanation could be that good grooming led to positive interactions and respect from others, which led to motivation and an overall pick-up in mood, and consequently in grades.

Intuitive Design and Ambience

The designer Victor Papanek has said of intuition, "design is the conscious and intuitive effort to impose meaningful order." This statement opens the door to the influence of intuition in design, hard to categorize yet impossible to ignore. Robin Hogarth's work, *Educating Intuition,* finds bridges between intuition and innovation:

> Like many abstract concepts, intuition is sometimes referred to in an off-hand and sometimes in an esoteric way. If it is to be a useful idea, probably we need to abandon both senses of the word. Intuition like dreaming is a subjective process familiar to everyone but impossible to represent objectively. Nevertheless, we can appreciate the impact by reviewing successful execution of complex tasks, quick understanding of ambiguous circumstances and the breakthroughs of discovery or innovation.

Intuition is widely applied in design yet hard to rationalize. A simple yet profound example from James Monsees, *Putting Intuitive Back Into Intuitive Design* suggests:

> Just as the early hominids could tell a stick was good for hitting things, a little exploration taught them to whittle it into a sharp point for stabbing or spin it to create friction to start a fire. They didn't immediately know these things, but getting there wasn't a huge leap, and the process happened naturally. The interface and overall experience design of your product can take the same approach, allowing your product to meet your users' needs through intuition and exploration.

We are conditioned to accept what is proven scientifically to be the truth. Yet we have experienced the tacit and unexplained value from experiences that are felt and processed intuitively. By attuning to ambience, we situate ourselves for untapped opportunities, sometimes in the form of breakthroughs that can augment and improve our efforts borne of the traditional and rational.

ELEVEN

Events

Conversations are best in person, one on one, and if the conversation is an important one, then it becomes an event. A dinner table with four to eight guests can keep the conversation flowing spontaneously. When the number increases to twelve, there comes a need for facilitation to ensure that everyone feels included in the gathering. A group of twenty-five to fifty becomes a party, and orchestration becomes even more important for any intimacy to exist—a master of ceremonies can make a positive difference. A gathering of a hundred to three hundred becomes a mini conference, like a wedding, where performance, speakers, chief guests, awards, become central. The design involves careful attention to detail, intimacy begins to wane, networking becomes a byproduct, although few know how to work a large group in a way that leads to valuable connections for future relationships.

A gathering beyond three hundred becomes a big conference, similar to a concert, festival or trade show, where speakers or performers take center stage with an audience; such events may stretch over a couple of days, and we enjoy such large gatherings for their splendour, like the Met Gala or the Davos Conference, once or twice a year. The preparation for such conferences runs into a couple of years, and their scale causes much to be at stake. Such large gatherings create room for smaller gatherings that sprout around the big event, like the parties at the Oscars.

Retreats, offsites, panel discussions and workshops, a vernissage or a book launch, can cover a few days. They are mainly agenda-brainstorm-and-activity-oriented, and in most cases the size does not exceed thirty-five to fifty. Annual partnership meetings, or global team meetings of large companies can involve a few hundred, yet they seldom run into a few thousand, like a concert or a big conference. Design, facilitation and deft execution are at the heart of such events.

An event is defined as something of importance—-a special occasion. Given the broadness of the term, and the range and types of events that can be designed, it becomes necessary to frame the personality of the event. I am in favor of defining an event as an experience that is designed to reside in memory as something special and important with takeaways that are beyond a well packaged swag basket. If we ask ourselves what is it that we enjoy most in an event, almost everyone would agree that they like: a meeting or conversation that leads to deepening an old relationship or starting a new one, a special setting or venue, a chance to share about oneself, an occasion to dress up, a total experience that is well-crafted, where food, decor, entertainment and activity come together. These ingredients can regale a party of one or a few thousand— the skill of designing an event, often termed as design DNA, applies to big or small events, but the distinction mainly lies in concept, design, execution or operations.

Those who are better at concept or design, may prefer one-on-one conversations and mid-size gatherings, possibly a mini conference or a well-crafted wedding or anniversary. And those with excellent operational skills with a delight for grandeur may prefer larger conferences backed by good architecture and design. Players with better skills in the small to mid-size category may team with bigger players to support smaller gatherings within a big carnival.

My sweet spot in events lies at the intersection of conversations held in smaller gatherings, high on craft, where each participant gets to play, partake and sparkle within a well-designed jewel box. Framed thus, the movable feast can travel from a one-on-one conversation to a mini conference and support bigger events through teaming and collaboration.

My Back Pages

> Half-wracked prejudice leaped forth
> "Rip down all hate," I screamed
> Lies that life is black and white
> Spoke from my skull. I dreamed
> Romantic facts of musketeers
> Foundationed deep, somehow
> Ah, but I was so much older then
> I'm younger than that now
> ~ Bob Dylan

I relate well to the topsy turvy logic of this old Dylan classic. I reflect upon my own back pages, my recollections that matter, and realize how important they are for what I carry forth. Our back pages anchor us. Like the Dylan song, in my youth, I was so much older then. Through self-awareness, experience, reflection and confidence, I'm younger now. Perhaps not in body, but in spirit.

An informal sense of hospitality ran deep in our family. We lived in the boonies, in a farming community at the edge of a forest. It was not unusual for friends to drive miles to visit us and stay for dinner, often sleep over and leave after breakfast. The food and drinks were plentiful, my job was to do the flower arrangements and set the table. Evenings would end with long-playing records, James Last and Herb Alpert songs would give way to our generation, with ABBA crooning, "can you hear the drums Fernando," amid a cacophony of chirping crickets in the dark.

It was a natural progression that led me to a career in travel and hospitality, planning upscale holidays and meetings for topflight clients. As part of my responsibilities, I would need to recce and partake in some of these activities to ensure faultless recommendations. My repertoire expanded from home cooked meals to sauerkraut and schnapps, listening to a Schubert lieder on a train, passing the Rhine with castles alit on hilltops, or learning to savor a warm Guinness with kippers, by the heath, sometimes in the morning.

The desire to climb the corporate ladder led me to a career in the communications field at a Fortune 500 company. My responsibilities covered a well-designed newsletter, presentations and events, such as VIP visits, product launches, important announcements and briefings, celebrations and complex joint venture conversations that needed special care as they involved negotiations, strategic alliances and sometimes disentanglement. The reputation of the company was sacrosanct, impossible to protect without well laid out communications that spoke of social responsibility. Finding the right tone between the message and the experience can be a challenge in large companies. Influencing in ways that shield the brand while being approachable enough to enlist communities is how relationships are built.

Jeff Bezos brought a refreshing change to meetings by shredding the powerpoint in favor of a thoughtfully-written six-page memo with real sentences and paragraphs for everyone to read in silence, before opening the floor to debate and dialogue. Business narratives are breaking new grounds with storytelling continuing to have its moment. Events without carefully articulated content can become fleeting. We live in an era where everything is instant. Alongside the fast pace, there is room for thoughtfully-curated, keepsake-worthy content. I recall ages ago, when I managed our corporate newsletter, there were clear boundaries between employee, trade-partner and customer communications. I stumbled upon a chatty customer letter that was written as an ode to a product. I decided to publish the chatty letter alongside an internal reward ceremony and an external trade-partner visit. Such mixing of stakeholders was seen as unconventional at the corporate office, yet I received a complimentary letter from the CEO for being creative—his message urged me to continue to keep readers interested.

Despite the early grounding, my talent for events really came of age in my career as an executive search consultant for senior level executives. Like Dylan's lyrics, I carried "romantic facts of musketeers" from my prior life into deep alleyways of one-on-one career conversations, tied to important outcomes with several million dollars at stake. Such consequential conversations are the pulse of important business decisions. My role forced me to build relationships. I was the connector between the aspirations of senior executives and companies where they could take their careers to new heights, by coming close to what E.B. White liked to call the "stable of giants." I helped bring the stable within reach of the executive.

Well-orchestrated conversations and trust were the cornerstones for success in the role. I quickly rose to become a trusted consigliere. As I reflect, my success in this field came from building deep bonds with those in the running for a new opportunity—I viewed them as individuals with dreams and potential beyond the client mandate. I became genuinely interested in their lives, often beyond what the client may have requested. Oddly, this became a reason for clients to trust me more. I could steer them towards deeper understanding and relationship-building. My approach was not one of mass outreaches, but deep, highly select encounters. In my entire career, I had very few surprises, where someone would decline a position at the last minute. I could usually anticipate this well in advance through insightful, all encompassing conversations. This placed me in the coveted position of a trustworthy confidante.

By taking a select, relationship-building approach, I would set up meetings, keeping in mind the culture, personalities and anticipated outcomes. The facilitation would involve one-on -one, well-designed conversations, followed by group interviews and onboarding. I would draw upon my hospitality underpinnings by designing the full experience, as one would a small convention, with personalized care and attention to detail.

A Week's Literary Sojourn

My mother could be difficult on the best of days. She was bright, educated, argumentative and cut out to do more than raise two children. She directed her unrealized potential by pushing my brother and me to our limits. Everything had to be done thoroughly with little tolerance for mediocrity. As with many such demanding parents, there were times when she was the best mother in the world. I could pursue a demanding career, thanks to her support with raising my son. When I moved him to Singapore for high school, we wanted to do something special for her as a thank you present. We decided on a short holiday in England and France. She was a literature buff and both countries were home to her favorite authors and playwrights. I had reasonable disposable income but not enough for first class—the experience had to be crafted within constraints.

London was a good place to start. We stayed at a small hotel near Portobello Road, close to the famous travel bookshop in the film, *Notting Hill*. Covent Garden was where we spent most of a day, with its deep ties to Dickens—the depressive strains from Oliver Twist were offset by Eliza Dolittle's merry chatter as a flower girl. It was a joy to see my mother unwind and reconnect with literature, particularly in the English countryside, Wordsworth's Lake District, Hardy's Dorset. The crowning glory was Stratford upon Avon after seeing *As You Like It*. It was a difficult, emotionally-charged visit to England, given my mother's high-maintenance personality, yet worthy of the investment for the happiness, however brief, we could bring her.

France was more mellow. We experienced Guy de Maupassant mainly in the *rive gauche*. Our visit to Paris ended with the Moulin Rouge. The cabaret wasn't the most appropriate choice for my mother and son, who was in his early teens, but they enjoyed the overall spectacle. Neither of them drank alcohol, so the champagne was only my pleasure to partake in.

Before we embarked on the sojourn, I was advised by well-intended friends to reconsider my decision. They felt it was a bit over the top and I could say thank you by buying an expensive gift or something else, lower maintenance, which would be easier to execute. The decision is among the best I ever made. My mother left us a few short years after the holiday and the memory is one we hold dearly. The Spanish greeting, *con buena salud,* says it well. We must strive to seize happiness when in good health.

Constructing the Jewel Box

The revenues were good and the future looked promising. I was planning our annual community event held every winter, and our VIP guest for 2012 was a leading entertainment company in Los Angeles. I was visiting the Beverley Hills Hotel, the well-known, historic pink palace with its swaying palms and valets dressed in the same iconic color. I was confirming reservations for the legendary Polo Room as a venue for our annual event. As I crossed the hallway, I saw a woman, blond, with barely-there makeup. There was something ethereal about her manner—not the usual stridency one encounters in famous, luxury hangouts. I had a meeting at the Polo Bar and found that the woman was headed in the same direction. When we reached the Polo Bar, she started playing the piano with the deftness of a concert pianist. She played wistfully, from the heart. I wondered if she would agree to play at our upcoming event, but I wasn't sure I could afford her.

During the break I went up to her and enquired if she may be willing to play at our event. She handed me a number and said that her husband was her manager and the decision-maker. I called her husband and to my delight they agreed to perform at our event. The personalized approach helped—she had a long list of Hollywood patrons and a register overflowing with bookings.

Our seven-course sit-down dinner had been beautifully composed. The thirty or so guests were assigned seating to balance the personalities, with a few speeches from VIP guests. I met the pianist to brief her in advance on the sequence of the nocturnes, to ensure that the scales punctuated the speeches at the right tone and blended into the courses and toasts with appropriate distribution of light notes and slightly heavy tunes. The evening ended with brandy and cigars on the patio. Just enough food and wine, soothing nocturnes, everyone was sober but high on stories and the experience. The valet rolled in the cars without any ado. It was a perfect jewel box event hosted in the private Polo Room of the Beverley Hills Hotel.

I have hosted fundraisers styled as fêtes, exhibitions, vernissages, formal themed dinners, breakfast briefings, interviews, and various photoshoots in some of southern California's most iconic properties -—The Roosevelt, The Beverly Wilshire, The Biltmore, The Island Hotel, Nobu Malibu, The Malibu Beach Hotel (where a guest could walk barefoot in a tuxedo), the Getty Villa, Cecconi's in West Hollywood, Spargo Restaurant and also galleries and museums like the Bergamot Station, LA Artcore, other LA icons like the LA Athletic Club, the rooftop gardens of the old Kyoto Grand Hotel and also Sushi bars like the Hamasaku, tucked away in a strip mall. Some of their sushi is named after famous movie stars like Jane Fonda and Robert De Niro, as celebrities are frequent diners at the restaurant. The library of events hosted by me through the course of my career is endless.

My emphasis has always been on the ambience, the orchestration, possible entertainment carefully woven into the conversation and speeches, the relationship-building, the service, the food and wine. The sidenotes including the invite and tying the loose ends after the event are vital to the construction of a perfect jewelbox event. The food and wine can be underwhelming without the rest in place. Peter Gay, the noted educator said, "the idea of style is infected with a central ambiguity: it must give information as well as pleasure. It opens windows on both truth and beauty—a bewildering double vista." Truth and beauty are as important to the setting as food and wine, for a successful event.

The Changing Face of the Epic Dinner

My more recent experiments with the sit-down dinner have involved improvising the epic thirteen-course French dinner with hipster food. While I lived in New York, our neighborhood in Bushwick was getting gentrified with new restaurants and wine bars alongside old mom and pop delis. I had a chance to experiment in one of the newly opened wine bars downstairs from my studio on Tompkins Avenue, where the appointed silverware could playfully accompany conversations punctuating a six-course meal. It is possible to enjoy Le Hamburger with a bottle of Chablis, and recount our favorite lines from Hemingway and Fitzgerald with imagined nicotine-infused walls. Paris itself is embracing a new face while maintaining the romance and poetics. Once known for pâté, entrecôte, escargot and foie gras, the medley of brown and white sauces is being replaced by pretty pink and green plates, with salmon and endive and who can forget the comic, lush turmeric orgies in Madame Mallory's *Hundred Foot* Journey. Improvisation is fun when you know the rules, as you know how to bend them. Without knowing the rules it can be hard to pull off a successfully-improvised event.

The Ultimate Retreat

"When men and mountains meet, great things are done," said William Blake. I felt a rush of emotions when I read the famous *New York Times* headline, some years ago: "Davos Without Davos." The tiny village in the Swiss Alps hosts world leaders and can become an eponym for meetings in mountain resorts. The lure of such a village is a total experience, regardless of whether you are a skier or mountaineer.

One of my earliest memories of a mountain retreat is a training I attended in my mid-twenties, in the Black Forest region of Germany. It was a basic customer service program but what created a vivid memory was the experience. The big glass resort nestled in the snow-covered mountains, a greenhouse with lush tropical plants, evergreen, in sharp contrast with the white landscape outside. We were so young. I would walk to the village square with my course mates who wore the shortest skirts and shorts, unfazed by the cold. They enjoyed showing off their scars from mountain adventures on well-toned legs. I also recall, most fondly, the presence of a beautiful Siberian cat. Languid and regal, he would curl up by the fireplace and take a leisurely walk outside, leaving paw-prints in the snow. I have attended many wonderful offsites and retreats, but what made this experience special was the ambience, the Davos-effect.

The presence of animals can enliven the retreat and set us in a frame of mind for the big picture, reconnecting our purpose with the business. My favorite animal interventions in retreats are breakfast with the chimps, horses and the presence of stables, a red barn with a barred owl, real reindeer crossings. Archetypes can deepen and mythologize an experience when designing a retreat:

Since the early 18th century, monks living in the snowy, dangerous St. Bernard Pass—a route through the Alps between Italy and Switzerland—Kept the canines to help them on their rescue missions after bad snowstorms. Over a span of nearly 200 years, about 2000 people, from lost children to Napoleon's soldiers, were rescued because of the heroic dogs' uncanny sense of direction and resistance to cold. Since then, through much crossbreeding, the Canines have become the domestic St. Bernard dogs commonly seen in households today.

~ Smithsonian Magazine

It was a beautiful spring day in 2016, when I met the Program Director for UC Berkeley's Executive Coaching Institute. The certification formed part of the Executive Education at the Haas School of Business. We met over lunch at a cafe in Larkspur, Marin County. Towards the end of our engaging lunch I decided to sign up to join their upcoming cohort. The experience was remarkable, situated at Berkeley's historic Faculty Club, surrounded by trees and near the clock tower—the clock chimed by the hour, adding to the character of the place. The curriculum was inspiring and the cohort, a talented group, were out to save the world. What stands out for me about the course is the emphasis on the performing arts, the curated readings, the theatrics, superb faculty and the ambience.

The Swag

We sometimes ignore the quality of the swag basket at retreats. Berkeley had picked high quality items, thoughtfully packaged, with a few edible treats, wine and a great selection of books.

I have sometimes advised clients not to co-brand expensive things in a swag or as corporate gifts. Gifts are an age-old way to spread cheer among employees and build ties with partners. Gift-giving is diplomacy 101. People seldom buy luxury items for themselves. A small spend of $500-1500, which may be part of the business budget, can go a long way in the world of gifts.

My early career in travel and hospitality did not offer a high salary but I received the most luxurious gifts—tulips from KLM, big floppy umbrellas with wooden handles from British Airways, Hediard chocolate and so much more. I would share these gifts with family and friends. As my corporate career progressed, I received luxury items as corporate, co-branded gifts. Companies would engrave their brand along with the luxury brand. I was pleased to receive such gifts, but limited in my ability to spread cheer. I would often say, ditch the engraving on the gift; that way, a Montblanc pen can travel from an aunt to a graduating nephew, for example. Instead, write a thoughtful note on art paper or a card, with the corporate logo. A handwritten, well-composed note with the gift is enough corporate branding. If you liberate the gift, your brand will travel further through the exchange of hands and the spreading of a story. Otherwise, it may languish in a forgotten heap on a desk or at the bottom of a closet.

In the course of my work I am often queried about the intersection of theory and practice. There is a common belief that theoretical translates into impracticality in real-life. My own experience has been to the contrary, possibly because I embraced theory intentionally after my years of real-life, practical experience. I was able to translate theoretical learnings for practical application through the design studio workshop approach.

The Design Studio Workshop

While at Berkeley, I came in touch with the firm IDEO. I was inspired by the impact their workshops had made in business, furthering innovation through creativity and design thinking. Having spent many years in corporate and entrepreneurial roles, I wished to reconnect with my innate creativity by designing a workshop that could take innovation to newer grounds. I decided to take my enquiry to Parsons School of Design, New York, pursuing graduate studies through a transdisciplinary selection of courses, covering fashion, architecture, media, design theory, anthropology, creative writing, visual and material culture, and philosophy. My thesis led to the Design Studio, a workshop in a studio format.

Having served some of the world's best companies, I was aware of the rising importance of innovation and creative thinking in business. I had practiced creative approaches in some of the most traditional companies and had been complimented for this tendency, earning myself the title of "out of the box thinker." Sharpening this skill at the world's best design school made perfect sense.

Acknowledgement of design's relevance in business is not new; the former IBM Chairman, Thomas Watson, famously said, "good design is good business." The challenge today is not as much in the "why" but more in the "how." Most traditional companies understand the value of creativity, but the barrier can lie in grappling with traditional systems, entrenched within old-fashioned thinking.

The Design Studio workshop offers a forum for ideation, reimaginings for breakthrough thinking and can also serve as a simple, fun-filled ice-breaker. The studio can be framed for a vast array of themes and outcomes. To arrive at the format, I studied various models and theories, including historical models that could be adapted for contemporary application.

A few historical influences include, *From Skills to Wisdom, Making, Knowing and the Arts* by Suzanne Butlers. Prior to the eighteenth century, the word "art" meant "skill," implying that any form of expertise could be learned. Butlers shares, "Aristotle's threefold division of knowledge into the theoretical, practical and the productive, embodied physical effort with enlightenment." The boundaries we have created between art and business can be blurred when we view art as skill.

Further observations include Pamela Smith's essay, *Making As Knowing: Craft As Natural Philosophy*. Smith calls attention to the informal alliance between art and science, describing the two as "vernacular sciences." Making with natural materials forced a knowledge of nature and generalized science. She shares that "craft can be investigative, like natural philosophy or science and not just productive." Such natural curiosity caused early craft methods to overlap with rudimentary science.

Suzanne Butlers adds, "from the maker's point of view, the physical act of making new things is predicated on empirical knowledge, but the very act of fabrication forces corporeal and intellectual spheres of activity." The Italian Renaissance enforced the practice of intellectual thought over physical manifestation in the studio. Michelangelo preferred to be known as Michelangelo Buonarroti, than Michelangelo the sculptor. By putting the brain above the brawn of carving marble, he could distinguish himself from the trade of sculpting and painting and maintain his status as a thinker and practitioner of fine art.

Ingenium refers to inborn talent that can be nourished by art. Improvisation can be construed as part of the arts yet improvisation extends into all human endeavors. Butlers shares that making can be understood "as a manifestation of empirical knowledge about the world but also to the delight in creating new things as a form of empirical knowledge about oneself. In it we directly experience the triad of nature, skill and inborn talent and respond creatively to it." The purpose of a studio approach to a workshop is ideation and discovery, as a group as much as individually. By taking an empirical approach to our innate talent paired with a workshop experience, we can create breakthroughs as seen throughout history. Such an argument translates to the designer becoming a change agent or a catalyst today.

The application of design beyond the realm of design is not a new one. As mentioned in the book *Design and the Creation of Value:*

> Inspired by Heskett's view of the designer as a change agent, something in tune with today's visually-oriented and instant and sharing new economy. The designer can be a modern industrialist-entrepreneur like Steve Jobs or Bill Gates. The designer can be a founder of the many social media and sharing economy firms that have emerged over the last number of years.

The protocol and format of the design studio workshop is informed by such historical research adapted for contemporary application. The propositional aspects of Design Studio offer examples themed along common business scenarios. An interdisciplinary approach allows a seamless investigation. One can think with one's hands and make with one's mind. History provides us with assurance that many contemporary boundaries are manmade and can be reframed for the relevant context. Our primal thirst for story and play can infuse the experience for better encounters, assimilation and recall.

IDEO's six steps for Design Thinking, a concept that they popularized through their workshops, include: Observation—Ideation—Rapid Prototyping—User Feedback—Iteration—Implementation. Against the six steps, a Venn diagram approach suggests that innovation happens at the intersection of feasibility, desirability and viability.

John Chris Jones's detailed treatise, *Design Methods* conceptualizes thirty-five methods for the design process. The methods broaden arguments to include everyday life and social encounters with design. Jones shares:

> The solution to a difficult problem, or the occurrence of an original idea will often come all of a sudden, the leap of insight and will take the form of a dramatic change in the way in which the problem is perceived, a change of set. The effect of this transformation is often to turn a complicated problem into a simple one.

Clarity that can emerge from entanglement with creativity makes room for experimentation at the Design Studio. Pertinent to the Design Studio is the application of synectics in the creative process. Shares Jones:

> We can regard Synectics as the feedback of black box output into black box input using carefully chosen types of analogy as instruments with which to transform output into input. It seems reasonable to expect that the use of analogies to which all members of the Synectics group contribute, will enable group members to share, to some extent, their capacity to re-pattern the original conflicting inputs until a pattern capable of resolving the conflict emerges.

At the human-centered level and with the increasing relevance of group participation in a design endeavour, while the creative leap or epiphany may come from one or two individuals intimately involved in the issue, it bears well to recognize that design is a group activity, and consequently the creative process can be democratized, even as one may defer to experts on the synthesis.

Methods for the Design Studio

The Design Studio's role as one of fostering innovation refers to the methods cited in John Chris Jones' book *Design Methods*. As an example:

John Chris Jones refers to John Page, a professor of building science, who proposes designers should adopt a cumulative strategy for design. Page's Cumulative Strategy involves increasing the time spent on analysis and assessment, keeping the two cumulative and convergent and reducing the time spent on synthesis of ideas that may turn out to be duds. The method makes it unnecessary to develop bad designs in order to learn how to develop good ones.

Steps for the cumulative stages include:

1. Outline of critical factors.
2. Identification of external factors that could become hurdles.
3. Define filters for unacceptable solutions.
4. Devise a method to test and validate each criteria.

Steps for the non-cumulative stages include:

1. An inventory of alternative plan B solutions for critical criteria.
2. Apply a sequence of tests to the sub-solutions, discarding those that fail.
3. Address design conflicts.

An example for this method could be an office setting that is being re-engineered or reconfigured and this could involve major changes in working, for example a move from independent offices to open plan. The variables are narrowed to work within the binding constraints and there could be less room for open-ended exploration.

This method enforces some level of expertise and reduces trial and error. This focused, directed approach facilitates execution and could become a platform for early elimination and value creation within a short time frame.

There are various methods cited by Jones that can be adapted for everyday business scenarios, some of these methods earmarked for the Design Studio approach include: Collaborative Strategy for Adaptable Architecture (CASA), Stating Objectives, and Removing Mental Blocks. Each of these approaches have been tested and offer frameworks that can be applied to a given business context.

Constructing with Scaffolding

Scaffolding and Constructing are important influencers for the Design Studio.

Scaffolding involves a teaching method that serves as a bridge to give students support and is designed to fade away as the student develops independent learning in the space.

Making activities for the Design Studio are aligned to the theory of Constructionism. Clinton and Rieber share:

> Constructionism suggests that learners are particularly likely to make new ideas when they are actively engaged in making some type of external artifact—be it a robot, a poem, a sand castle, or a computer program—which they can reflect upon and share with others.

The Influence of Bauhaus

The Bauhaus as an influencer for the Design Studio includes the unifying purpose of all creative disciplines under one roof in order to form a total work of art: a *Gesamtkunstwerk*. Further, the Bauhaus influences the nonhierarchical position of the Design Studio. The workshop was the structural basis of the Bauhaus method of teaching. Bauhaus founder, Walter Gropius, suggested that teachers be called masters and students be referred to as apprentices and journeymen so they may be placed in the context of real-world trades. Each workshop was shared by two teachers: *a workshop master,* typically a craftsman skilled in manual skills, materials, and production, and a *master of form,* generally a fine artist who would try to stimulate creative thinking. In *Foundations for Design Education: Continuing the Bauhaus Vorkurs Vision,* Fern Lerner writes:

> In Bauhaus fashion, design scientists would probably agree that the best universal, aesthetic language for multivariant problem-solving, could be learned through sequential, guided Vorkurs exercises. Students from K-12 might explore, play, discover, and creatively evolve a knowledge base, so that future cultural forms could emerge as a collective Gesamtkunstwerk.

An Example of the Design Studio Format

Day One (half a day)
A kick-off on a Thursday or Friday afternoon with introductions.
Some light craft activity, linked to the reading, as an icebreaker.
A short post-dinner discussion of the next day's assignment.

Day Two (Full day)
Making and thinking exercises, concurrent with story and play.
Feedback sessions on the craft and telling.
Potential to address feedback through making and thinking in a pre-dinner session.

Day Three (Full day)
Similar to day one but with a raised bar to improve conditions for a creative leap and creative challenge.
Conclusion with feedback at the end of the day,
pre-dinner or the next morning after a post-breakfast session.

The Design Studio can be shortened to a day or half a day, based on the context, goals and deliverables of the assignment. It is important to note that the success of the studio relies heavily on prework, to enable a better outcome within a short timeframe.

Design Studio Use Case

A company in the middle of a restructuring is soliciting feedback and looking for creative solutions with discretion, including a low threshold for risk and failure given the competitive environment, yet would like to bring external stimulus and break a linear course of decision- making. The context is tense and could use some lighthearted intervention.

Method suggested: Page's Cumulative Strategy, a making approach using structure, similar to Lego Serious Play or Drawings with anecdotal sharing. Anecdotes and stories could have participants practice role play to ease tension. Curated readings could include, strategy/game, problem-solving, cultural sensitivity, diplomacy. A discreet venue could include a conference room in an old club house. A thoughtfully-curated and tightly managed participant list. Appropriate documentation to ensure confidentiality.

Scaffolding could include conversations with the coach/facilitator, that have broader implications for senior leadership, critiqued by others in the group. This could create a thoughtful interplay of conversations. Constructing would involve groupwork at the workshop. The design of the workshop would mimic a Bauhaus in the making or craft within a total experience of readings and sharing of examples.

Follow up would include references from the workshop that may have been effective for the restructuring. Good outcomes could lead to continuity with coach follow-ups.

In closing, traditional companies who base their performance on incremental innovation can become stuck in designing what is referred to as a better mousetrap. By creating a whitespace outside the frames of traditional thinking, the Design Studio creates grounds for experimentation with transformational thinking, replacing the "mousetrap" with something new and better. Internal efforts can benefit from the external stimulus offered by the Design Studio.

At its base, the Design Studio offers a fun-filled format for engagement, team building, storytelling and ideation, without disrupting existing good momentum, should radical change or forced innovation be unnecessary.

Postscript

This book took many years in the making. When I finally decided to pen down my thoughts, it became an out of body experience. I had to shed my present and dance a slow waltz on the Blue Danube of memories. Such transcendence was only possible by reengaging with the senses, the agony and the ecstasy of relived moments, often impossible to capture in the straightjacket of language.

Reliving deeply felt experiences and translating them into wise nuggets for the present brought me in touch with myself from a distance, akin to a virtual reality experience where I was once handed a VR headset to unite with a tree. My senses were transported and became one with the tree—I could hear the tree grow, crackle and sprout leaves, even smell the bark and the earth. My body elongated with the tree's trunk on its journey upwards. It was an intimate, humbling and cathartic experience. I felt a similar connection with my deepest self, my soul, as I wrote this book.

The famous literary axiom attributed to Tolstoy says that all literature falls into two categories: "a man goes on a journey or a stranger comes to town." This is true of life, too. As we weave our life's literature, we go on a journey. I am very far from where I was born. The apple has traveled far from the tree on a journey of discovery and I have been halted on my tracks with business closures, by disruption. I am familiar with the proverbial "stranger who comes to town". I know them as the phantom of hurdles, disrupting life's course.

There is more ecstasy than agony in rising up again, celebrating the gift of life and reweaving all the dreams for a new day. Designing experiences for a meaningful life is a worthy cause. I offer my life in the service of others, to help with designing meaningful experiences, like the weaver bird, deft and persevering.

In the following pages I have included further reading and experiences that have been influential for me (by no means exhaustive, just a sampling) as an extension of my own thoughts. Thank you for your interest in my book, and I hope that our paths cross again in person.

Further Reading and Experiencing

One: Communication

1. Asaro, Peter, *Killer Robots & the Ethics of Autonomous Weapons*
https://www.youtube.com/watch?v=O7v5utK-fHA

2. Day, Ray, *The Future of Your Corporate Reputation*
https://www.prweek.com/article/1921639/future-corporate-reputation

3. Frontline, *The Persuaders*
https://www.pbs.org/video/frontline-persuaders/

4. Harari, Yuval Noah, *Nexus: A Brief History of Information Networks from the Stone Age to AI*
https://www.amazon.com/Nexus-Brief-History-Information-Networks/dp/059373422X

5. Lockyer, Peter and David Thaxton *Interview: chat about Les Mis*
https://www.youtube.com/watch?v=EDRGXK0QJys

6. McLuhan, Marshall predicts *'world connectivity'*
https://www.cbc.ca/player/play/video/1.3593404

7. Russell, Bertrand, *Mankind's Future & Philosophy*
https://www.youtube.com/watch?v=gvOcjzQ32Fw

8. Words
https://radiolab.org/podcast/91725-words

Two: Goodbye

1. Castaneda, Carlos, *The Teachings of Don Juan: A Yaqui Way of Knowledge:*
https://www.goodreads.com/book/show/78250.The_
Teachings_of_Don_Juan

2. Cohen, Leonard, *Hey, That's No Way to Say Goodbye*
https://www.youtube.com/watch?v=b-bJPmasXKs

3. Capaldi, Lewis, *Someone You Loved*
https://www.youtube.com/watch?v=zABLecsR5UE

4. Green, William, *Richer, Happier, Wiser-Conversation with Chris Davis, Berkshire Hathaway Director*
https://www.theinvestorspodcast.com/richer-wiser-happier/
learning-from-warren-buffett-
harlie-munger-w-chris-davis/

5. Say it with Flowers
https://www.youtube.com/watch?v=e2lQ10CZRUU

6. Two Harbors for Walks
https://www.visitcatalinaisland.com/about-the-island/two-
harbors

7. Workplace ESG: How ESG Factors Shape Employee Engagement
https://www.greatplacetowork.com/resources/blog/workplace-
esg-environmental-social-governance-employee-experience

Three: Kintsugi

1. Attias, Richard, *Interviewed on Saudi TV*
https://www.youtube.com/watch?v=efQQTZrSHGo

2. Burton, Richard, *talks about Elizabeth Taylor*
https://www.youtube.com/watch?v=xA8ifRFS0-0

3. Davis, Paul, *Go Crazy*
https://www.youtube.com/watch?v=nhu3orNqZu4

4. Eagles, *Strange Locations. Glenn Frey House, Don Henley House, Linda Ronstadt House Laurel Canyon*
https://www.youtube.com/watch?v=RH61tPpw1JI

5. Gates, Bill, *Opens Up About Divorce And Infidelity Accusations*
https://www.youtube.com/watch?v=7T87-aGadwM

6. Gaga, Lady, *House of Gucci Interview*
https://www.youtube.com/watch?v=oICch4aoIyA

7. Kemske, Bonnie, *Kintsugi, The Poetic Mend*
https://www.amazon.com/Kintsugi-Poetic-Mend-Bonnie-Kemske/dp/1912217996

8. Kintsugi: Broken is Beautiful
https://www.youtube.com/watch?v=ym3XO5VsvMw

9. Koren, Leonard, *Wabi-Sabi: for Artists, Designers, Poets & Philosophers*
https://www.amazon.com/Wabi-Sabi-Artists-Designers-Poets-Philosophers/dp/0981484603

Four: Style

1. Aarons, Slim, *A Wonderful Time: An Intimate Portrait of the Good Life*
https://www.amazon.com/wonderful-time-slim-aarons-Books/s?k=a+wonderful+time+slim+aarons&rh=n%3A283155

2. Allen, Woody, *Annie Hall*
https://www.youtube.com/watch?v=Bj4ZoeRMHwU

3. Beldegreen, Alecia, *The Bed*
https://www.amazon.com/Bed-Alecia-Beldegreen/dp/1556701802

4. Chariots of Fire
https://www.youtube.com/watch?v=1eYGl8PNjlU

5. Dherbier, ann-Brice (Editor), Pierre-Henri Verlhac (Editor)
Jackie: A Life in Pictures
https://www.amazon.com/Jackie-Life-Pictures-Yann-Brice-Dherbier/dp/1576872424

6. Hart, Alexandra Jacopetti, *Radical Acts: Native Funk & Flash*
https://www.youtube.com/watch?v=qeuFznem7jA

7. Look@Work
https://www.lookatwork.lu/fr

8. Penman, Phil, *Street Scenes*
https://www.philpenman.com/publications/8-phil-penman-street-scenes/

9. Serrat, Joan Manuel, *De Vez en Cuando la Vida (Actuación RTVE)*
https://www.youtube.com/watch?v=7x4sShxhE38

10. The Great Gatsby
https://www.youtube.com/watch?v=4w8lohkQtbY

11. The Last Tango in Paris
https://www.youtube.com/watch?v=o35Z4ue0BP

Five: Incidentals

1. 30 Years of ASSOULINE
https://www.youtube.com/watch?v=I3O_XHFeEBA

2. Art with Jim - Cezanne's Still Life
https://www.youtube.com/watch?v=JsD6NoAuby0

3. Delibes: Lakmé - Duo des fleurs (Flower Duet), Sabine Devieilhe & Marianne Crebassa
https://www.youtube.com/watch?v=C1ZL5AxmK_A

4. Gaiman, Neil, *Discusses His Writing Method (Which He Doesn't Recommend)*
https://www.youtube.com/watch?v=KYaQEpX8d0k

5. Halston: Inventing American Fashion
https://www.amazon.com/Halston-Inventing-American-Lesley-Frowick/dp/0847843491

6. Jean-Luc Godard's CONTEMPT Trailer
https://www.youtube.com/watch?v=Yyr2GSXucw0

7. Kale Salad | easy, beautiful salad recipe
https://www.youtube.com/watch?v=ISCELWuLEIc

8. Shakespeare and Company - Iconic Bookshop in Paris
https://www.youtube.com/watch?v=1k1VV1j_k08&t=9s

9. The Postcolonial Euphoria of Malick Sidibé's Photography | Collection in Focus
https://www.youtube.com/watch?v=2HrmUAI-WIw

Six: Luxury

1. Darling
https://www.youtube.com/watch?v=Hz8wPq_vJyM

2. Fashion and Everyday Life: London and New York
https://www.amazon.com/Fashion-Everyday-Life-London-York/dp/1847888267

3. Ford, Tom, *Spring 2011 Fashion Show*
https://www.youtube.com/watch?v=cipuNKK9dms&list=RDMM&index=13

4. HOUSE TOUR | Inside a Stylish Apartment at the Iconic Carlyle Hotel
https://www.youtube.com/watch?v=6fWu9-LoieE

5. PRADA presents "A THERAPY"
https://www.youtube.com/watch?v=-gl-kaGumng

6. RALPH LAUREN | Polo Ralph Lauren | Le Tour De Paris With Emma Chamberlain and Pierce Abernathy
https://www.youtube.com/watch?v=dm2unwKfEZU

7. Sakul Intakul HOW-TO ep. 2 'LOTUS SQUARE' Modern Asian
https://www.youtube.com/watch?v=V3ND1MMkr6Q

8. The Waldorf Astoria, a hotel that defined hospitality, is reborn
https://www.youtube.com/watch?v=MjN8NBvqv_U

9. Tiffany & Co. — "Some Style is Legendary" Documentary
https://www.youtube.com/watch?v=AvS0f6jTbp4

10. VALLEY OF THE DOLLS 1967 | NYC Filming Location | Martha Washington Hotel
https://www.youtube.com/watch?v=cYRNVcUGyVg

Seven: Loss

1. Bellow, Saul, *Herzog*
https://www.youtube.com/watch?v=FLYIHuIQhAM

2. Carnegie, Dale, *How to Win Friends & Influence People*
https://www.amazon.com/How-Win-Friends-Influence-People/dp/0671027034

3. Frankl, Viktor, *Man's Search for Meaning*
https://www.youtube.com/watch?v=_t-YGGUytno

4. Green, William, The Inner Scorecard w/ Pico Iyer
https://podcasts.apple.com/ae/podcast/rwh055-the-inner-scorecard-w-pico-iyer/id928933489?i=1000699326627

5. Im, Saroeup, *How I Survived the Killing Fields: A Story of Hope, Love and Determination*
https://www.amazon.com/How-Survived-Killing-Fields-Determination/dp/0978946219

6. I'll Be Your Mirror
https://www.youtube.com/watch?v=KGZWb1SIiR4

7. Moorer, Allison, *A Soft Place To Fall* https://www.youtube.com watch?v=rju2AO4tB_M&list=RDMM&index=15

8. Fiddler on the Roof
https://www.youtube.com/watch?v=kDtabTufxao

9. Thúy, Kim, *Ru*
https://www.amazon.com/Ru-Novel-Kim-Th%C3%BAy/
dp/1608198987

10. Y&R Star Eric Braeden Makes Emotional Return to Home
Lost to LA Fires (Exclusive)
https://www.youtube.com/watch?v=cAoQwc78J0I

Eight: Playtime

1. Erdei, Peter, old-world craftsmanship
https://erdeidesigns.com/the-furniture/

2. How To Make a Paper Boat That Floats - Origami Boat
https://www.youtube.com/watch?v=khuVGbCE0PY

3. Kelley, Tom and David Kelley, *Creative Confidence: Unleashing the
Creative Potential Within, Us All*
https://www.amazon.com/Creative-Confidence-Unleashing-
Potential-Within/dp/038534936X

4. Nobili, Simone, *Lizard Life*
https://www.amazon.com/Lizard-Life-Mr-Simone-Nobili/dp/
B0FBLMXC2N

5. Pearce, Simon
https://simonpearce.com/pages/our-story

6. Top 6 Fruits Decoration Ideas / Super Fruits Decoration /
Fruit-carving & cutting hacks
https://www.youtube.com/watch?v=hXq5CLAWFaA

7. von Busch, Otto, *The Design Comedy: The Descent Through Inferno*
https://www.setmargins.press/books/the-design-comedy-
designs-decent-through-inferno/

8. Watercolour doodles Human figures
https://www.youtube.com/watch?v=cHilWMjGlWs

Nine:Reboot

1. Chip Conley, *Midlife is a Chrysalis, Not A Crisis*
https://podcasts.apple.com/us/podcast/midlife-is-a-chrysalis-not-a-crisis-chip-conley/id582272991?i=1000641285807

2. Busta, Kevin
https://www.kevinbusta.com/c-v

3. Hughes, Robert, *The Shock of the New*
https://www.youtube.com/watch?v=h-NnoZg7MDE

4. Lewis, C. S. *A Grief Observed*
https://www.amazon.com/Grief-Observed-C-S-Lewis/dp/0060652381

5. Miracle Worker
https://www.youtube.com/watch?v=RH601NY6Kf0

6. Music of the Heart
https://www.youtube.com/watch?v=Qz78YTyOTmA

7. Nevins, Mark D. and John Hillen and *What Happens Now?: Reinvent Yourself as a Leader Before Your Business Outruns You*
https://www.amazon.com/What-Happens-Now-Reinvent-Yourself-ebook/dp/B07BFH4XC8?ref_=ast_author_mpb

8. Schrager, Ian on *Consistently Capturing the Zeitgeist*
https://www.youtube.com/watch?v=3-VxluY1kgk

9. Sáinz-Villegas, Pablo, *Spanish Romance*
https://www.youtube.com/watch?v=2wnLgR9jxWo

10. Watch Koko the Gorilla Use Sign Language in This 1981 Film | National Geographic
https://www.youtube.com/watch?v=FqJf1mB5PjQ

11. Uribe, Kirmen, Bilbao-New York-Bilbao:
https://www.goodreads.com/book/show/28006401

Ten: Ambiance

1. Amazon Wildlife In 4K - Animals That Call The Jungle Home | Amazon Rainforest | Relaxation Film
https://www.youtube.com/watch?v=AhP5Tg_BLIk

2. Cabaret
https://www.youtube.com/watch?v=EfL1J4QVhSM

3. Cabanne, Pierre, *Dialogues With Marcel Duchamp*
https://www.amazon.com/Dialogues-Marcel-Duchamp-Capo-paperback/dp/0306803038

4. Kandel, Eric, *Memory and the Work of Art*
https://www.youtube.com/watch?v=u8MQxma9-Uo

5. Klute
https://www.youtube.com/watch?v=cB4JB8kECFk

6. Nature Is Speaking – Julia Roberts is Mother Nature
https://www.youtube.com/watch?v=WmVLcj-XKnM

7. Turner, Alwyn, *Biba: The Biba Experience*
https://www.amazon.com/Biba-Experience-Alwyn-W-Turner/dp/185149541X

8. Wagner's last overwhelming opera
https://www.youtube.com/watch?v=3pN_e0ZNBs0

9. Wilson, Elizabeth, *Bohemians: The Glamorous Outcasts*
https://www.amazon.com/Bohemians-Glamorous-Outcasts-Elizabeth-Wilson/dp/0813528941

Eleven: Events

1. Arts: Counterpoint | The New York Times
https://www.youtube.com/watch?v=BixPLIWcb0s

2. Cards on the Table
https://www.allbirds.com/pages/cards-on-the-table

3. Churchill, *Henrietta Spencer, Classic Entertaining:*
https://www.goodreads.com/book/show/691441

4. Greystone Mansion | Beverly Hills Wedding
https://www.youtube.com/watch?v=NmPatUovxqA

5. Heavenly Luxury Picnics
https://www.youtube.com/watch?v=ZaoFfd2Xa7E

6. How To Make A Classic Mint Julep | GQ
https://www.youtube.com/watch?v=TSUwaDhhxiU

7. Jaffrey, Madhur, *Indian Cooking*
https://www.amazon.com/Madhur-Jaffrey-Indian-Cooking/
dp/0764156497

8. Jiro Dreams of Sushi
https://www.youtube.com/watch?v=0VB_DrsHDQ0

9. Meyer, Danny, *Setting the Table: The Transforming Power of
Hospitality in Business*
https://www.goodreads.com/book/show/213280.Setting_the_
Table

10. Paris Society
https://www.youtube.com/watch?v=xB5xP-aBE9M

11. Ross, Patt, Formal Country Entertaining
https://www.amazon.com/Formal-Country-Entertaining-Pat-
Ross/dp/0670838098

12. Wanders, Marcel and Andaz Amsterdam, *Celebrating Creative
Luxury*
https://www.youtube.com/watch?v=UvXhNx-R04c

13. When Attitudes Become Form: Bern 1969/Venice 2013
https://www.youtube.com/watch?v=fNbLNgf35_4

Bibliography

Ackerman, Diane, A Natural History of the Senses, Vintage Books, 1991

Aesthetics Research Lab https://aestheticsresearch.com/ 09/19/2025, 11:50AM

AIGA https://www.aiga.org/, 09/19/2025, 11:51AM

Allende, Isabel, In the Midst of Winter, Simon Schuster, 2017

Angelou, Maya, Goodreads, https://www.goodreads.com/ quotes/5934-i-ve-learned-that-people-will-forget-what-you-said-people Accessed, 09/14/2025, 1:52 PM

Aristotle and Bartlett, Robert, Aristotle's "Art of Rhetoric," University of Chicago Press, 2019

Arrein, Angeles. The Four Fold Way. Harper Collins, 1993

Auden, W.H. "September 1, 1939," Michael Sheen https:// www.youtube.com/watch?v=Ol8w3L04I8U Accessed, 09/14/2025, 2:05 PM

Bagley, Chris, Behind Comme des Garçons is Zen-Loving Contrarian, Bloomberg https://www.bloomberg.com/news/ articles/2014-10-07/behind-comme-des-garcons-stands-zen-loving-contrarian-ceo?embedded-checkout=true Accessed 09/15/2025 4PM

BBC, Dunbar's Number: Why we can maintain only 150 relationships? https://www.bbc.com/future/article/20191001-dunbars-number-why-we-can-only-maintain-150-relationships 09/14/2025, 4:56PM

Baudelaire, Charles, The Ragpickers' Wine, <https://www.poetryfoundation.org/poems/54376/the-ragpickers-wine Accessed 09/15/2025>, 4PM

Baum, Frank, The Wonderful Wizard of Oz, Penguin, 1995

Bergdorf Launches Holiday Windows, "Toast of the Town" celebrates flagship store's Fifth Avenue locale, https://vmsd.com/bergdorf-launches-holiday-windows/ Accessed 09/15/2025 8:24PM

Berkeley Executive Coaching Institute, https://www.berkeleyeci.com/, Accessed, 09/17/2025, 12:16PM

Bezos, Jeff, No Powerpoints - All meetings center around 6-page memo, https://www.youtube.com/watch?v=L227qFemjqI, Accessed, 09/17/2025, 11:35PM

Blake, William, Goodreads, https://www.goodreads.com/quotes/10353116-great-things-are-done-when-men-and-mountains-meet-this Accessed, 09/17/2025, 12:09PM

Bloomberg, Mergers, Breakups and the Battle for Content, https://www.bloomberg.com/news/videos/2025-07-13/mergers-breakups-and-the-battle-for-content-video Accessed, 09/14/2025, 4:26PM

Blumberg, Jess, A Brief History of the St. Bernard Rescue Dog, Smithsonian, https://www.smithsonianmag.com/travel/a-brief-history-of-the-st-bernard-rescue-dog-13787665/, Accessed, 09/17/2025, 12:12PM

Bouttell, Laura, What Leadership Style is Jamie Dimon? Complete Analysis <https://quarterdeck.co.uk/articles/what-leadership-style-is-jamie-dimon 09/14/2025>, 6:15PM

Boyle, Brendan, 6 Ways to Integrate Play Into the Workplace, https://www.inc.com/author/brendan-boyle, Accessed, 09/16/2025, 11:44AM

Britannica, Discours sur le style, Georges-Louis Leclerc, count de Buffon https://www.britannica.com/topic/Discours-sur-le-style, Accessed 09/14/2025 5:40PM

Britannica, Dizzy Gillespie https://www.britannica.com/biography/Dizzy-Gillespie, Accessed 09/14/2025, 5:56PM

Brooks, Amanda, I Love Your Style, iT Books, 2009

Brown, Pauline, Aesthetic Intelligence: How to Boost It and Use It in Business and Beyond, Harper Business, 2019

Burke, Theta, "Learnings of the Heart,"Sounds of Yourself, Delafield Press, 1977

Butters, Suzanne, From Skills to Wisdom: Making, Knowing, and the Arts', in P. H. Smith, A. Meyers, & H. Cook (Eds.), Ways of Making and Knowing: The Material Culture of Empirical Knowledge. Ann Arbor, Mich: University of Michigan Press, 2014, pp. 48-85, Accessed, 09/17/2025, 12:50PM

Camillus. John, Strategy as a Wicked Problem, HBR, <https://hbr.org/2008/05/strategy-as-a-wicked-problem 09/15/2025>, 1:00PM

Carroll, Rory, The fall and rise of the Gucci empire, The Guardian https://www.theguardian.com/g2/story/0,3604,376489,00.html Accessed, 09/14/ 2025, 4:30PM

Center for Disease Control and Prevention, https://www.cdc.gov/nchs/fastats/deaths.htm, Accessed, 09/16/2025, 11:17AM

Chabbott, Sophia, Luxury's Lament: The End of Flaunting, WWD https://wwd.com/fashion-news/designer-luxury/feature/luxurys-lament-the-end-of-flaunting-2071562-1510118/ 09/15/2025 2:30PM

Clinton, Gregory and Lloyd Rieber, The Studio Experience at the University of Georgia: an example of constructionist learning for adults, Educational Technology Research and Development, Dec.2010, vol.58, Issue 6, pp 755-780.

Clifford, James, The Predicament of Culture: Twentieth-Century Ethnography, Literature, and Art, Harvard University Press, 1988

CNN, What is Maslow's hierarchy of needs? A psychology theory, explained https://www.cnn.com/world/maslows-hierarchy-of-needs-explained-wellness-cec, 09/15/2025, 12:30 PM

Cohan, George, Always Leave Them Laughing When You Say Good-Bye (1903) https://www.youtube.com/watch?v=0n1TOTmEUoU, Accessed 09/14/2025 3:37 PM

Cohen, Leonard, Boogie Street https://www.youtube.com/watch?v=n6wdRLuzPJ0, Accessed 09/15/2025, 8:45PM

Cohen, Leonards, Famous Blue Raincoat, https://www.youtube.com/watch?app=desktop&v=ohk3DP5fMCg&feature=youtu.be, Accessed 09/16/2025, 12:08PM

Colette, Chéri, Random House, 2001

Conley, Chip, The Value of Collective Effervescence in Experience Design Futurespaces https://futurespaces.com/recordings/the-value-of-collective-effervescence-in-experience-design, 09/15/2025, 3:23PM

Conley, Chip, The Midlife Chrysalis, https://www.meawisdom.com/podcast/, 09/18/2025, 8:45PM

Conway, Daniel, Margaret Thatcher dress and the politics of fashion, The International Politics of Fashion, Andreas Behnke, Routledge, 2017

Crawford, Kelly, Fashion as Tigersprung https://www.linkedin.com/pulse/fashion-tigersprung-kelly-crawford/ Accessed 09/15/2025, 11AM

Crowe, Lauren Goldstein, and Sagra Macera de Rosen, The Towering World of Jimmy Choo / A Glamorous Story of Power, Profits, and the Pursuit of the Perfect Shoe, Bloomsbury, 2009

Culler, Jonathan, Theory of the Lyric, Harvard University Press, 2015

Davos without Davos, https://www.nytimes.com/2022/01/16/business/davos-world-economic-forum.html, Accessed, 09/17/2025, 12:00PM

Dalrymple, William, "The Song of the Holy Fools," The Guardian, 06 Feb. 2004

De Beauvoir, Simone, Letters to Sartre, Arcade Pub, 1992

De Niro, Robert, A Bronx Tale https://www.youtube.com/watch?v=v77Dj4FhIA8, Accessed 09/15/2025 4:26PM

Dr. Zhivago, Frozen Heaven, https://www.youtube.com/watch?v=8aBmdAmBYtw Accessed 09/15/2025 11:50 AM

De Saint-Exupéry, Antoine The Little Prince, Harcourt Inc, 2000

Desiderata https://www.sfu.ca/~wainwrig/desiderata.htm, 09/15/2025 1:04PM

Draper, Don, Mad Men https://www.reddit.com/r/quotes/comments/1waxwu/in_greek_nostalgia_literally_means_the_pain_from/ Accessed, 09/15/2025, 11:13AM

Drucker, Peter, Gooreads, https://www.goodreads.com/quotes/59441-the-most-important-thing-in-communication-is-to-hear-what Accessed, 09/14/2025, 1:50 PM

DW History and Culture,1970: This photo of a German chancellor went down in history. Why? https://www.youtube.com/watch?v=W7iVNoWDJDY, Accessed 09/14/2025, 4:36PM

Dylan, Bob, My Back Pages, https://www.youtube.com/watch?v=92cF_KCH7TU , Accessed, 09/17/2025, 10:53PM

E! Why Bill Gates Regrets Divorcing Melinda French Gates | E! News https://www.youtube.com/watch?v=HOvVKdRvMHc 09/14/2025 5:08PM

Eberle, Scott, The Elements of Play Toward a Philosophy and a Definition of Play, https://www.museumofplay.org/app/uploads/2022/01/6-2-article-elements-of-play.pdf, Accessed 09/16/2025, 11:35 AM

Emerson Ralph Waldo, Goodreads, https://www.goodreads.com/quotes/259136-insist-on-yourself-never-imitate-your-own-gift-you-can, Accessed 09/14/2025, 6:26PM

Eugene McKendry, Storytelling Myths and Legends, Northern Ireland Learning, BBC https://www.bbc.co.uk/northernireland/schools/11_16/storyteller/pdf/gen_notes_all.pd Accessed, 09/14/2025, 2:32 PM

Fekkai, Frederic, A Year Of Style, Clarkson Potter Publishers, 2000

Fekkai Life https://fekkai.com/pages/thefekkailife, Accessed 09/14/2025 6:41PM

Ford, Tom https://www.youtube.com/watch?v=cK2V8yhCeRo Accessed 09/15/2025 3:12PM

Fry, Tony, Urban Futures in the age of Unsettlement, Elsevier, 28 January 2011, 433

Gaiman, Neil The View From the Cheap Seats, William Morrow 2016

Gay, Peter, Style in History, W. W. Norton & Company, 1989

Gentleman's Journal, The style lessons you should learn from the Godfather, https://www.thegentlemansjournal.com/article/style-lessons-godfather-coppola-suit-gangster-style-menswear/ Accessed 09/14/2025, 6:18PM

Gissler, Glenn, RIGHT NOW https://www.youtube.com/watch?v=2KGZEwnk9Go, Accessed, 09/16/2025, 3PM

Green, William, Richer, Wiser, Happier: How the World's Greatest Investors Win in Markets and Life, Scribner, 2021

Gucci, https://www.gucci.com/us/en/nst/history-of-gucci?srsltid=AfmBOoqb

Gucci, https://www.gucci.com/us/en/nst/history-of-gucci?srsltid=AfmBOoqbMu0G0fZkI5kmlgtDhezJi35xEyvF6kSmYygzT7ogxohJU557, Accessed, 09/18/2025, 9:11PM

Gun Violence Data and Research, https://oag.ca.gov/ogvp/data, Accessed 09/16/2025, 11:20AM

Gusto The Manager Mass Exodus: How SMBs Are Flattening the Org Chart https://gusto.com/resources/gusto-insights/managerial-flattening-2025, Accessed 09/15/2025 7:16PM

Harvard Health Publishing, The secret to happiness? Here's some advice from the longest-running study on happiness https://www.health.harvard.edu/blog/the-secret-to-happiness-heres-some-advice-from-the-longest-running-study-on-happiness-2017100512543 Accessed 09/14/2025 4:52 PM

Hale, Thomas, "Griots and Griottes," Indiana Press, 1998

Harrigan, Diane, "Rakugo and Japanese Culture, Something Old and Something New" https://muse.jhu.edu/pub/5/article/850475/pdf, Accessed 09/14/2025, 2:26 PM

Hawoldar, Shakuntala, You, Mauritian Poetry, 1981

He, Quiliang, "Between Business and Bureaucrats, Pingtan Storytelling Maoist and Post Maoist China," Sage Journals, March 22, 2010

Henley, William Ernest, Invictus, https://www. poetryfoundation.org/poems/51642/invictus, Accessed 09/15/2025, 9:10PM

Heller, Bernard, The 100 Most Difficult Letters, Harper Collins, 1994

Heskett, John, Design and the Creation of Value, Bloomsbury, 2017

Høeg, Peter, Smilla's Sense of Snow, Random House, 1995

Hollander, Anne, Sex and Suits, Alfred A. Knopf, 1994

Hollies, Bus Stop https://www.youtube.com/ watch?v=It75wQ0JypA, Accessed 09/15/2025, 6:53Pm

Hughes, Melissa, The Neuroscience of Color, https://info.variquest.com/blog/the-neuroscience-of-color, Accessed, 09/16/2025, 2:55PM

Hughes, Robert, The Shock of the New, Thames and Hudson, 1991

Huppatz, D.S. Revisiting Herbert Simon's Science of Design, Massachusetts Institute of Technology, Design Issues, Spring 2015

IBM, https://www.ibm.com/history/architecture, Accessed, 09/17/2025, 12:34PM

IDEO, Creative Confidence, https://www.ideo.com/journal/ creative-confidence, Accessed, 09/15/2025, 12:30PM

Ilchi, Layla, Tiffany & Co. Reveals Campaign for Pharrell Williams' 'Titan'
Jewelry Collection, WWD https://wwd.com/fashion-news/fashion-scoops/pharrell-williams-tiffany-titan-jewelry-campaign-1236408203/ Accessed 09/15/2025 4:20PM

Institute of Labor Reforms, Tort Costs In America, US Chamber of Commerce, 2024

Invictus, https://www.youtube.com/watch?v=vKzrv-pbmGc, Accessed, 09/14.2025, 04:39PM

Irving, Washington, Rip Van Winkle, Black Dome Press Corp, 2003

Johnson, Diane, Christine Lagarde: Changing of the Guard, Vogue, Magazine, August, 22, 2011

Jones, John Chris, Design Methods, Wiley, 1992

Jaques Elliott, Death and the Mid-Life Crisis, Routledge, 1988

Kawakubo, Rei Comme des Garçons: Art of the In-Between, https://www.youtube.com/watch?v=VVXv8tJFUGc 09/15/2025 8:30PM

Keats, John, Ode On A Grecian Urn, Poetry Foundation https://www.poetryfoundation.org/poems/44477/ode-on-a-grecian-urn Accessed 09/14/2025 4:05 PM

Kipling, Rudyard, Lichtenberg, Kiplingsociety https://www.kiplingsociety.co.uk/poem/poems_licht.htm Accessed 09/14/2025, 4PM

Kirkbride, Robert, Architecture and Memory:
The Renaissance Studioli of Federico da Montefeltro (Gutenberg-e), Columbia University Press, 2008

Koch, Howards, Casablanca, Script and Legend, The Overlook Press, 1992

Lee, Andrew, Creating Spontaneity: The Evolution of the Samsung Group Under Lee Kun-Hee, Wesleyan University https://digitalcollections.wesleyan.edu/_flysystem/fedora/2023-03/23925-Original%20File.pdf 09/15/2025, 8:00PM

Lee Emery, "Believing in Artistic Making and Thinking,"Studies in Art Education, Vol. 30, No. 4 (Summer, 1989), pp. 237-248 Published by: National Art Education Association Stable URL: https://www.jstor.org/stable/1320260 , Accessed, 09/16/2025, 12:00PM

Lerner, Fern, Foundations for Design Education: Continuing the Bauhaus Vorkurs Vision,Studies in Art Education, Vol. 46, No. 3 (Spring, 2005), 211-226

Levi Primo, Survival In Auschwitz, Simon & Schuster, 1996

Levine, Davis, 3 Ways Lego Serious Play Will Transform Your Meetings and Workshops, DXD Digital, Oct. 26, 2017

London School of Hygiene and Tropical Medicine, Expert Comment: Loneliness impacting 1 in 6 people, WHO report finds, https://www.lshtm.ac.uk/newsevents/news/2025/expert-comment-loneliness-impacting-1-6-people-who-report-finds, Accessed 09/15/2025 7:20PM

Loro Piana, https://www.laconceria.it/en/luxury/leather-goods-push-loro-piana-dont-call-us-quiet-luxury/ Accessed, 09/15/2025, 2:24PM

Mahatma Gandhi Arrives in the U.K. (1931) | British Pathé https://www.youtube.com/watch?v=P6njRwz_dMw, Accessed 09/14/2025, 4:44PM

Maison Martin Margiela, (9/4/1615) - Museum Boijmans Van Beuningen 1997, https://saint-martin-bookshop.com/products/maison-martin-margiela-9-4-1615-museum-boijmans-van-beuningen-1997 Accessed 09/15/2025 4:06PM

Markham, Edwin, Goodreads https://www.goodreads.com/quotes/8703-he-drew-a-circle-that-shut-me-out--heretic-rebel Accessed 09/15/2025, 9:07PM

Masefield, John, Goodreads, https://www.goodreads.com/quotes/94910-the-days-that-make-us-happy-make-us-wise, Accessed, 09/18/2025, 8:39PM

McCluhan, Marshall, "The Medium is the Message" https://web.mit.edu/allanmc/www/mcluhan.mediummessage.pdf Accessed 09/14/2025, 2:35 PM

McDowell, Erin, "How Ray Kroc built McDonald's from a small burger joint into a global fast-food empire,"Business Insider, Accessed 09/14/2025 3:17 PM

Mezrich, Ben,"He Thinks We're Going to Take a Swing at Him?": Inside the Decades-Long Cage Match Between Mark Zuckerberg and the Winklevoss Twins," Vanity Fair, https://www.vanityfair.com/news/2019/04/inside-the-mark-zuckerberg-winklevoss-twins-cage-match?srslti d=AfmBOopzYRAFS8qqB_C0gf77JVq0Nr-wA69w0JqHn5TUL5O6gMI3Y3ew Accessed 09/14/2025 3:30 PM

Meares, Hadley, Crazy Love: Elizabeth Taylor and Richard Burton's Epic Romance, Vanity Fair, https://www.vanityfair.com/hollywood/2020/08/elizabeth-taylor-richard-burton-marriage-furious-love?srsltid=AfmBOoqQXbshvsY6kbhm4siwAb-RyMRkDWHQq470reZSiq_Fzy90Vji9 Accessed 09/14/2025, 5:12PM

Merter, Sevi, Synesthetic Approach in the Design Process for Enhanced Creativity and Multisensory Experiences, The Design Journal, 20:sup1, S4519-S4528, DOI: 10.1080/14606925.2017

Milne, A and Shepard E, Winnie-the-Pooh, Dutton Books for Young Readers, 1988

Monsees, James, Putting Intuitive Back Into Intuitive Design,UX Magazine, October 14, 2014 https://uxmag.com/articles/putting-intuitive-back-into-intuitive-design, Accessed, 09/16/2025, 3:04PM

Mother Teresa, Who was Mother Teresa? https://www. youtube.com/watch?v=BTd1EcT_vvY, Accessed 09/15/2025, 12:20 PM

Nietzsche, Friedrich Aphorisms on Love and Hate, Penguin Classics, 2015

Officer, Donald, The Unexpected Relationship Between Intuition and Innovation,
The Public Sector Innovation Journal, volume 10 (3), article 35. https://pdfs.semanticscholar. org/9427/16accd12236449ebb9572b5091c59a4b66b1.pdf, Accessed, 09/16/2025, 3:10PM

Papanek, Victor, Design for the Real World, Human Ecology and Social Change, Academy Chicago Publishers 1984 embed, 09/15/2025, 12:40PM

Parsons School of Design https://www.newschool.edu/ parsons/?utm_source=google &utm_medium=cpc&utm_campaign= TNS_Search_Text_Parsons_Brand&gad_source=1& gad_campaignid=931654278&gbraid=0AAAAADfsqW jmdRynobmDcd05mwc JETD1z&gclid=Cj0KCQjw_ rPGBhCbARIsABjq9ccVm33pKIVJi_uqX KODkdYWV_kX-WAPSav7ttbK_7vwDJZaVLzdG2caApMzE ALw_wcB,
09/19/2025, 11:54PM

Peter Pan, Goodreads, https://www.goodreads.com/quotes/ tag/peter-pan, 09/18/2025, 9:22PM

Pew Research Center, https://www.pewresearch.org/short-reads/2023/10/12/what-does-friendship-look-like-in-america/, 09/18/2025, 9:10PM

Poe, Edgar Allen, The Fall of the House of Usher, Goodreads https://www.goodreads.com/quotes/504815-during-the-whole-of-a-dull-dark-and-soundless-day Accessed, 09/14/2025, 4:21 PM

Priestly, J.B. Bright Day, Reprint Society Ltd, by arrangement with William Heinemann Ltd, 1948

Prince Charles meets Gerry Adams, https://www.youtube.com/watch?v=_SZGPlhhQa8, Accessed, 09/14/2025. 4:48PM

Proust, Marcel A literary legend: The life and legacy https://www.youtube.com/watch?v=WD_QCYHvlOk Accessed, 09/15/2025 8:16PM

Reuters World's priciest chocolate goes on display in Portugal https://www.reuters.com/article/lifestyle/worlds-priciest-chocolate-goes-on-display-in-portugal-idUSKCN1GS26O/ Accessed, 09/15/2025 3:32PM

Rhino Factoids The Eagles Reunite, Hell Freezes Over https://www.rhino.com/article/rhino-factoids-the-eagles-reunite-hell-freezes-over, Accessed 09/14/2025, 4:17 PM

Roff, Don, Goodreads, https://www.goodreads.com/author/quotes/847186.Don_Roff?page=3, Accessed, 09/16/2025, 4:22PM

Ross, Diana, "Sorry Doesn't Always Make It Right," https://www.youtube.com/watch?v=PBz_KL8HMNc Accessed, 09/14/2025, 3:04 PM

Schiaparelli, Elsa, Shocking Life, E.P Dutton & Co.Inc, New York, 1954

Sidney, Philip, "The Defence of Poesy,"Goodreads, https://www.goodreads.com/quotes/23555-the-poet-he-nothing-affirmeth-and-therefore-never-lieth Accessed 09/14/2025 2:13 PM

Shakespeare, William, Julius Caesar, https://poets.org/poem/julius-caesar-act-ii-scene-i-it-must-be-his-death-and-my-part/embed, 09/15/2025, 12:40PM

Shakespeare, William, Macbeth, https://www.poetryfoundation.org/poems/56964/speech-tomorrow-and-tomorrow-and-tomorrow, Accessed 09/15/2025 1:02PM

Shakespeare, William, A Midsummer Night's Dream, https://www.poetryfoundation.org/poems/58139/speech-bottoms-dream, Accessed, 09/16/2025, 2:32PM

Shaw, George Bernanrd, Philosiblog, https://philosiblog.com/2012/01/06/the-single-biggest-problem-in-communication-is-the-illusion-that-it-has-taken-place/accessed, 09/14/2025, 1:44 PM

Smith, P, Ways of Making and Knowing: The Material Culture of Empirical Knowledge, https://www.jstor.org/stable/jj.20261350, 09/17/2025, 12:45PM

Socrates, Goodreads https://www.goodreads.com/quotes/452128-to-know-thyself-is-the-beginning-of-wisdom, Accessed 09/14/2025. 6:28PM

Sorkin, Michael, Exquisite Corpse: Writings on Buildings, Verso Books, 1994

Stamp, Jimmy, Who Really Invented the Smiley Face? Smithsonian Magazine https://www.smithsonianmag.com/arts-culture/who-really-invented-the-smiley-face-2058483/ 09/15/2025, 7:36PM

Stouffer Hotels Commercial (1985), https://www.youtube.com/watch?v=k6gEJZSNGbs, Accessed, 09/15/2025, 9:22PM

Taylor, Edward, Edward Tylor's concept of Animism https://www.sociologyguide.com/anthropology/edward-tylors-concept-of-animism.php Accessed 09/15/2025 8:05PM

The Guardian, The Rise and Fall of French Cuisine https://www.theguardian.com/news/audio/2019/jul/29/the-rise-and-fall-of-french-cuisine-podcast, Accessed, 09/16/2025, 11:00AM

The Hundred Foot Journey, https://www.youtube.com/watch?v=fZ7XRCnsThM, Accessed, 09/17/2025, 11:56

Tolstoy, Leo, Goodreads https://www.goodreads.com/quotes/57886-all-great-literature-is-one-of-two-stories-a-man, Accessed, 09/16/2025, 3:42PM

Tolstoy, Leo, Anna Karenina, Goodreads, Penguin Classics, 2004

Trachtenberg, Jeffrey Ralph Lauren: The Man Behind the Mystique, Little Brown Company, 1988

Twain, Mark, Goodreads, https://www.goodreads.com/quotes/646569-find-a-job-you-enjoy-doing-and-you-will-never, Accessed 09/16/2025, 11:28PM

von Busch, Otto, Drawn to Fear: A Fashion Action and Drawing Book, SelPassage, 2017

Van Deijnen, Tom, visiblemending <https://visiblemending.com/products/tom-of-holland Accessed 09/15/2025> 4:30PM

W Magazine Remembering Anne Slater, a Legendary Fixture of New York City Society https://www.wmagazine.com/story/anne-slater-dies-new-york-socialite-remembrances, Accessed 09/14/2025, 5:53PM

Wagner's last overwhelming opera https://www.youtube.com/watch?v=3pN_e0ZNBs0 09/15/2025, 4:38PM

Wallace David Foster, This Is Water https://www.youtube.com/watch?v=DCbGM4mqEVw Accessed 09/15/2025 7:03PM

Walt Whitman https://ca.pbslearningmedia.org/resource/american-vid-walt-whitman/video/ Accessed 09/15/2025 7:24PM

Ward, David, Forever Young: The Existential Style of Jack Kennedy, Smithsonian <https://npg.si.edu/blog/forever-young-existential-style-jack-kennedy Accessed 09/14/2025> 6PM

West, Melanie, Hotel-Style Hospitality Comes to Hospitals, https://www.wsj.com/articles/hotel-style-hospitality-comes-to-hospitals-11544968800?gaa_at=eafs&gaa_n=ASWzDAhRizLpdUXmYL-ONQkxIwwDLaLbQFr240qIy-asArZqtm3hGqJZa7SXPOayhOs%3D&gaa_ts=68c9dbf7&gaa_sig=2qW0YkvB0teqMfDPY6ZuYQ-v_SdH41J1ofdjhmj4FWFq FQi1YM9NAFMKMKJ1dYq-96mBKTmqsr9SgN57lijV4A%3D%3D, Accessed, 09/16/2025, 2:41PM

White, E.B. Here Is New York, The Little Bookroom, 2000

Wiesel, Elie, Do Nothing, That's Being Dead, https://medium.com/the-1000-day-mfa/do-nothing-thats-being-dead-182ddd7b5e5e Accessed 09/15/2025, 11:10AM

Williams, Raymond, Culture is Ordinary, 1958 https://www.people.iup.edu/sherwood/Courses/ENGL480S06/Documents/Williams_Culture_Is_Ordinary.pdf Accessed 09/15/2025 9:00PM

Winterson, Jeanette, The Power Book,, Vintage, 2001

Wordsworth, William, I Wandered Lonely as a Cloud, https://www.poetryfoundation.org/poems/45521/i-wandered-lonely-as-a-cloud,, Accessed 09/16/2025, 11:25AM

Young, Robb, Christine Lagarde: Dressing All The Way To The Bank, BBC

Zadie, Smith Killing Orson Welles At Midnight https://www.nybooks.com/articles/2011/04/28/killing-orson-welles-midnight/ Accessed 09/15/2025, 8:41PM

Zilber, Ariel, Workers making more than $100K laid off at alarming rate as number of US millionaires plummets https://nypost.com/2023/08/16/richcession-six-figure-earners-laid-off-at-three-times-rate-of-low-income-americans/ Accessed 09/15/2023 7:12PM

Romasha Nath curates and designs workshops and events. She was formerly an executive search consultant and advisor to Fortune 500 companies. She now coaches emerging leaders on how to become better communicators by designing meaningful experiences.

Romasha began her career in the travel and hospitality industry before joining the communications field and progressing her consulting career. Romasha is a graduate of Parsons School of Design in New York and a certified coach from UC Berkeley's Haas School of Business.